stashwith**splash**
quilts

CINDY CASCIATO

KRAUSE PUBLICATIONS
CINCINNATI, OHIO

www.fwmedia.com

14 13 12 11 10   5 4 3 2 1

DISTRIBUTED IN CANADA BY FRASER DIRECT
100 Armstrong Avenue
Georgetown, ON, Canada L7G 5S4
Tel: (905) 877-4411

DISTRIBUTED IN THE U.K. AND EUROPE BY DAVID & CHARLES
Brunel House, Newton Abbot, Devon, TQ12 4PU, England
Tel: (+44) 1626 323200, Fax: (+44) 1626 323319
Email: postmaster@davidandcharles.co.uk

DISTRIBUTED IN AUSTRALIA BY CAPRICORN LINK
P.O. Box 704, S. Windsor NSW, 2756 Australia
Tel: (02) 4577-3555

Library of Congress Cataloging in Publication Data
Casciato, Cindy.
    Stash with splash quilts / by Cindy Casciato. -- 1st ed.
        p. cm.
    Includes index.
    ISBN-13: 978-0-89689-811-0 (pbk. : alk. paper)
    ISBN-10: 0-89689-811-3 (pbk. : alk. paper)
    1. Patchwork--Patterns. 2. Quilting--Patterns. 3. Appliqué--Patterns. I. Title.
    TT835.C39174 2010
    746.46--dc22   2010006383

Edited by Liz Casler and Kelly Biscopink

Designed by Julie Barnett

Production coordinated by Greg Nock

Photography by Ric Deliantoni and Christine Polomsky

metric conversion chart

TO CONVERT	TO	MULTIPLY BY
inches	centimeters	2.54
centimeters	inches	0.4
feet	centimeters	30.5
centimeters	feet	0.03
yards	meters	0.9
meters	yards	1.1

ABOUT THE AUTHOR

Cindy Casciato (pronounced Cash-auto) is a teacher, designer, author and most importantly, a quilter with thirty years of experience teaching quilting and related topics to numerous guilds and organizations. Her first quilt publication titled *Block Explosion* was released by Leisure Arts in the fall of 2004. Her second publication titled *One Stitch Quilting: The Basics* was released by KP Books in the spring of 2006. Cindy has her own line of patterns printed under her label, "Threads of Friendship." You can visit her website at www.friendshipthreads.com.

She is the founder of the very successful Quilt Escape, a quilter's retreat held every year since 1994, and has been able to reach thousands of other quilters and keep the circle of friendship growing. Learn more at www.quiltescape.com.

Cindy was the National Education Manager for Jo-Ann Fabrics for eight years. She was the designer of the American Spirit Quilt Kit for the Patriots Day Project in June of 2002. Working with the American Sewing Guild, she presented quilts to fire departments nationwide.

Cindy has been married to the same wonderful man for forty years. She and Drew have four children and three grandchildren, all of whom reside within a 25-mile radius of their home in Ravenna, Ohio.

Cindy is available for group programs and workshops. You may contact her at cindyquilts@neo.rr.com or cindyquilts@quiltescape.com for more information.

DEDICATION

As always, there are those behind the "seams" that make all the difference in our lives. I am exceptionally blessed to have Drew Casciato, a wonderful husband of 40 years. We are a team. Together we have raised four children and now we have the time to travel together meeting quilters all over the country. Thanks to his constant encouragement I have been able to quilt and write when I needed to do it. He is a fabulous cook and loves to create something new in the kitchen so I often have more time to quilt than I know what to do with. He knows when I am at my wit's end and is there to get me back on track, such as letting me know when a design is good or bad. He has a great sense of color. Maybe that has something to do with listening to my color lecture a hundred times or more. Probably not, as he usually tunes me out during lectures. Anyway, as husbands go, I know I have the best one.

Thank you, Drew, for your love and support and here's to the years ahead.

ACKNOWLEDGMENTS

I would like to thank my wonderful friend, Claudia Bissler from the Calico Hearts Quilt Guild of Ravenna, Ohio. Without her support and encouragement this book would not be possible. She has given me countless hours of piecing time, not to mention the fellowship of sewing together. It was such a pleasure to be in my studio on the days that Claudia came to sew.

Many thanks to Krause Publications and especially Candy Wiza for their belief in my concept of utilizing stash fabric with new splash fabrics. In addition I would like to express my admiration and respect for a wonderful lady, Nancy Zieman, who has done so much to advance sewing and quilting in our lives.

My special thanks go out to all my longarm quilting friends, Kay Wilson, Janis Hittle, Eva Birch, JoAnne West and Nancy Gano, who have contributed their time and talents to my quilts.

contents

DEAR QUILTING FRIENDS,

I'm so pleased and excited that you have chosen my book, *Stash with Splash Quilts*. Inside this book you will find an immense variety of patterns, most with more than one version and quilt size. There are some new piecing and appliqué techniques for you to try when making my stash plus splash quilt recipes.

While nothing in this book could be considered rocket science, I think you will find that my style of keeping things simple will help you to complete more quilts in less time. If I had to describe my own personal style of quilting I would have to say, "More quilts in less time make me a happy girl." After almost thirty years in quilt making I have made over three hundred quilts. My mantra is simply Keep it Simple, Make it Colorful and Make it Quick.

I spend a lot of time writing directions and I'm always interested in the processes of rotary cutting, piecing and quilt assembly. Fewer steps in a process give me more quilting time to enjoy. So, please don't skip the general instructions where I introduce my magic triangle method. It was such a simple discovery but the end result is outstanding. Also in this book is an amazingly fast method of machine appliqué that I hope you will try.

Stash, stash, stash! Do you have any stash? What's all the fuss about anyway? Now that you know I have been quilting for quite a while, I guess you know my stash is out of control. This overwhelming need for fabric is definitely an obsession. Do you think I may need counseling? I have organized and reorganized these fabrics so many times I can't count them. I have bought many different containers to sort and store this stash as well. My husband, Drew, a very patient man, has indulged me by building a 15-foot counter with large shelves underneath just to store my stash containers. For many years I sorted this stash by colors and types of fabric. Yipes! You guessed it—I actually started out sewing garments, making dolls, drapes and other household items. Once my four children grew up, I gradually converted to making quilts more than anything. My latest organizational system is to sort by color (for fabrics that fit into a color category, like solids or blendables) or by fabric style. My style categories are Americana or patriotic, 1930s feed sack, Civil War, batik, novelty or conversational, large floral prints, stripes, dots, plaids, backing, etc. Now that I've gone on record and admitted to having this huge amount of stash fabric, let me say that at some point I realized that it might be a good idea to plan more quilts that incorporate my stash. Hence, the idea of *Stash with Splash Quilts* came to me as a method of dipping into my stash piles and at the same time allowing me to continue to enjoy new splash fabrics.

Splash, splash, splash! Who are you kidding? You can't stop buying fabric! Stop feeling guilty and start combining that stash with new splash fabric with my fun, fast, fantastic quilt patterns. You really will have fun running off to your favorite quilt shop where your quilting friends can help you select just the right splash fabrics to work with your stash and make your quilt oh so special. Have fun!

I hope you will enjoy the process as much as the end results.

In stitches,
Cindy

Stash and Splash Fabrics

STASH OR SCRAP

What is the difference between stash fabric and scrap fabric? Scrap fabrics are pieces smaller than ¼ yard and stash fabrics are those fabrics ¼ yard or more just waiting to be auditioned for your next quilt. Some of your stash may be fabrics left over from other projects as well as some that haven't even been cut into. Either way the recipes in this book call for stash fabric amounts between ¼ yard and a couple of yards.

SPLASH FABRICS

Splash fabrics are those special pieces of fabric that we sometimes refer to as the zinger—the wow fabric that brings a quilt together. Splash fabrics are tie-together prints that unify and intensify. I like to make blocks from my stash fabrics at home (and who knows how old that stash really is) and go to my favorite quilt shop to locate just the right splash fabric to pull all my blocks together.

HOW TO PLAY WITH SPLASH AND STASH FABRICS

1. Pick the project that you want to make. Look over the yardage requirements to see how much stash and splash you need.

2. Pay attention to where in the quilt each of the stash and splash fabrics goes. You will notice that in most cases the blocks are made mostly from the stash fabrics. Sometimes there's a piece of splash fabric in

Pulling it all together

Have fun making blocks and using up your stash fabric. Then enjoy a trip to your favorite quilt shop to purchase that special splash fabric that will pull your project all together.

the blocks to tie it into the overall design, such as in the quilt *Dancing Leaves*. In other cases, the entire body of the quilt is made from stash, and the splash appears only in the borders, as in the quilt *Trip to Amish Country*. Finally, one more way to incorporate the splash fabric into your quilt is via appliqué. Many large scale floral fabrics lend themselves to the cutout motif method that I describe in the *Garden Star* project.

3. Now it's time to get out your stash containers and begin sorting through the piles. Set aside the stash fabrics that you want to play with.

4. Once you've chosen your stash fabrics, you have a couple of options. Option 1: Take your book and the stash piles to the quilt shop and play. Option 2: Make a block from your stash first and then take it and your book to the quilt shop.

5. Lay out the block or piles of stash fabric on top of the bolts of fabric at the quilt shop. Stand back at least five feet to see how the fabrics work together. If you have a pair of binoculars, take them with you and reverse them so you get the faraway view. Does the splash fabric jump out at you? Are there any fabrics that no longer seem to work together? The right splash fabric will help you to see all the colors/fabrics in the quilt, while at the same time pause to enjoy the excitement of the pattern and colors in the splash fabric.

6. Keep playing until you are satisfied that you have the right splash fabric that pulls your project together. Then go home and get sewing!

Organizing Your Stash

So, let's get started! Go to your stash bins, containers or baskets and start by sorting your stash fabrics. Clear off any large table or counter to work on. In a pinch, you can set up a couple of ironing boards to arrange the fabrics. Depending on the amount of your fabric stash, this process may take a while. But I guarantee that the time saved on the project end of the process will be worth the time spent organizing. Here's how I like to sort:

- Place any fabric piece smaller than ¼ yd. into a scrap basket.

- Take 34 pieces of typing paper and write one of the colors or styles listed below on each paper. These styles are a good starting point. As you inventory your fabric stash you may find other fabric styles not listed. Please make up your own styles as you find them in your stash.

Blendables or Solids:
These fabrics are easy to classify as one specific color.

- Yellow
- Yellow-Orange
- Orange
- Red-Orange
- Red
- Red-Purple
- Purple
- Blue-Purple
- Blue
- Blue-Green
- Green
- Yellow-Green
- Black
- White
- Gray
- Brown
- Beige/Cream

Styles:
These fabrics usually combine several different colors into one design, making it difficult to sort them into a specific color family.

- Americana/Patriotic
- 1930s Feedsack Reproduction
- Civil War
- Batiks
- Novelty/Conversational
- Large Florals/Focus
- Stripes
- Dots
- Plaids/Checks
- Backing
- Baby/Juvenile
- Christmas/Holidays
- Landscape (e.g. rocks, trees, sky, water)
- Paisley
- Fleece/Flannels
- Foliage
- Animals

OK! You've finally got all your fabric sorted. Take a look around you. Is this exciting or what? Now it's time to make some decisions based on how much storage space you have. I outgrew the classic under-counter storage system. I didn't want to reveal that in the intro letter because I thought you might think I was truly obsessed! Actually, I outgrew my original sewing studio as well and it has been converted into a home office. I moved into our basement and took it over. In my old space, I had very large containers crammed so full I could barely lift them out of the shelves onto the table to sort. Now I have smaller containers sorted into more colors and styles. This makes it much easier for me to find the fabrics I want to work with. I typed labels on my computer and printed them out. The labels really make it easy to find the fabrics very quickly. My bins are small and easy to lift over to a table for sorting. This system really works for me and I hope it works as well for you.

1

techniques:
sew simple methods for successful results!

Through years of piecing and quilting, I have discovered many shortcuts along the way. My favorite techniques are included in this book. In this chapter, you will learn about my magic triangle method. If you don't like to rotary cut ⅛" strips, squares or triangles, you will love this method. The best part of these tips and tricks is that most of the tools used are basic things you already have on hand.

Cutting Out Setting Triangles

Setting triangles are needed in quilts with diagonal sets. They are usually cut from a square by making two diagonal cuts across the square. However, as you begin to set blocks that are nine inches or more, the square becomes too large to cut out on a standard mat, so it's much easier to cut these triangles from a strip.

USING A REGULAR RULER

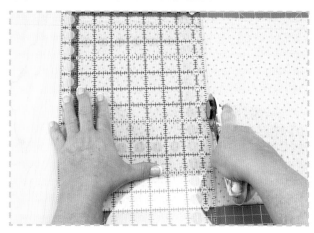

1 Cut a strip of fabric the width indicated by the project instructions.

2 Place the 45-degree line of a 6" × 24" ruler on the long side of the strip. Cut the first angle.

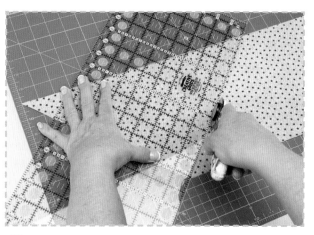

3 Continue to flip the ruler along the outside edge of the strip, placing the 45-degree line on the long side. Line up the ruler with the last cut to create a 45-degree setting triangle. Notice that the grain runs along the long side of the triangle.

The triangles complete the edge of the row when you sew the quilt top together.

NOTES FROM NANCY

Before cutting triangles, consider spray starching and pressing the fabric. The starch adds stability to the fabric, which is especially helpful when seaming the bias edges of the triangles. I recommend using non-aerosol spray starch.

Sewing a Scant ¼" Seam Allowance

What's the fuss about? Isn't ¼" always ¼"? Technically it may be a true ¼" seam. However, when you're piecing, a little more than a ¼" seam allowance is taken up when you press the seams to one side. The best test I have come up with is sewing three strips together and measuring across the seams for the results.

I prefer to use a shorter stitch length when piecing quilts. Generally, I set my machine at 12–15 stitches per inch. The shorter stitch length secures the starting and ending of the seams in lieu of old-fashioned backstitching. A shorter-stitch length is a great insurance policy!

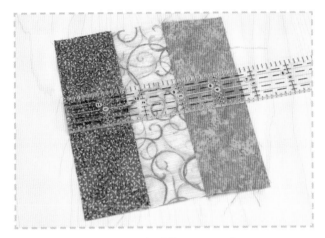

The width should be a precise 5".

Sew a scant ¼" seam allowance.

1 Simply cut out three 2" × 5" long strips and sew them together on their long sides. Press the seams out from the center.

2 Measure across the width of the patch and it should measure 5" making the patch a perfect square. If this is not the case, you may have discovered that your ¼" seam is just a little too wide . To correct this you will need to sew a scant ¼", which is just inside the ¼" mark. Many times, using your standard presser foot and altering the needle position will give you exactly what you want. The nice thing about using the standard presser foot is that it is made to align perfectly with the feed dogs on your machine. This makes a big difference when you are feeding strips, squares or triangles under the presser foot. You can also compensate for a wide ¼" seam by pressing your seams open.

Pressing Seams

Pressing seams makes all the difference in the accuracy of the blocks.

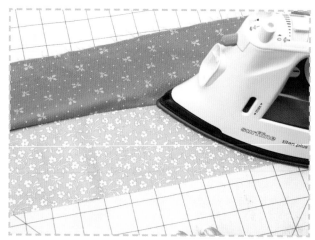

1 Set the seam by pressing down on the wrong side of the fabric with the side of the patch or strip facing you that you want to push over (usually the dark side is wrong side up).

2 Once you set the seam, flatten the seam from the right side of the fabric by using the nose of the iron to push the seam allowance toward the darker fabric.

Thread-Pinning Method

Thread-pinning is a method of joining patches in a continuous chain without cutting the threads between the patches. This method works for any block that is joined together in rows. The example below is a nine-patch block. I love this method because it keeps all my patches in the correct order. It often makes a difference in the outcome of the block if a patch gets turned around. The thread-pinning prevents this from happening.

Chain-sewing is a method of sewing many similar patches in a continuous feed without cutting the threads between the patches. This method can be used in many of the patterns in this book. Play some music as you sew and enjoy the process.

1 Assemble the patches of your block and lay them in rows. Make sure all the patches are arranged to look like your block diagram. Flip the patches in the center column to the left, right sides together, on top of the left column patches. Start from the top of the left column and place the patches under the presser foot.

2 Chain-sew your first two patches together making sure they match at the intersections. Pick up the next pair of patches and butt it against the previous pair. Continue to sew across the next patch. They will be connected with a single thread. Finally add the third pair in the row.

3 Use the end of your seam ripper to guide the patches under the presser foot and to prevent them from shifting. I can usually use this tool instead of pinning.

4 Open up the first two patches in each of the three rows. Start at the top of row three in your layout and place the patch right sides together on top of the center patch in the row. Instead of pinning, use your seam ripper to help you guide the patches under the presser foot. Stitch across each patch in the row keeping the bottom edges butted closely together.

5 Open the rows up across the block. You now have three rows sewn together and linked by a thread. There's no way to accidently turn a patch the wrong way as they are all joined in order.

6 Press the seams in alternating rows in opposite directions. For instance, if you press the center row seams toward the center patch, then you would press the top and bottom rows away from the center patch. This will set the block up for perfectly opposing seam allowances.

7 To finish the block, fold the top row right sides together with the center row and stitch across the seams. Use the point of your seam ripper to push the seams in opposing directions. Open up the block to check for seam alignment.

8 Working on the wrong side of the block, use the nose of the iron to push the seam allowances from the center row to the outside rows. Turn the block over to the right side and flatten the seam.

Magic Triangle Method

HALF-SQUARE TRIANGLES

How much time do you spend rotary-cutting strips, squares and triangles? How much easier would it be to cut with a measurement of 2" or 2½" compared to 2⅛"? I know finding the ⅛" measurement line on any rotary ruler can be frustrating at best. In fact, I'm sure that's why I'm wearing bifocals now—just kidding. You know what I mean, though—it's so much faster to place the ruler on the 2½" line rather than the 2⅛" line. Change is not always easy, but this time it's easy and sew much fun. From this point on you will not need to cut any strips, squares or triangles with an ⅛" measurement. Hurrah! Here's how to skip the ⅛" measurements in any future projects.

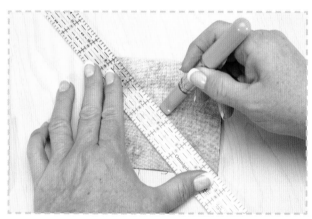

1 Using a marking pencil or chalk wheel, draw a diagonal line on the wrong side of one of the two squares to be pieced together. Layer the marked squares right sides together with the other square.

2 The secret is in the sewing. You need to sew ³/₈" from the drawn line on both sides. Some presser feet are ³/₈" from the center of the foot to the outside edge. Check to see if yours is. If not, shift the needle position to find an accurate ³/₈" seam. Once you've done that, align the edge of the presser foot with the drawn line. Sink the needle into the patch before you start to sew to prevent threads from tangling. Use the point of your seam ripper to help guide the patch under the presser foot.

A NOTE ON MEASUREMENTS

For every half-square triangle patch you make, add 1" to the finished size. Example: A 3" finished square plus 1" seam allowance equals 4", a very easy round number to rotary-cut. Under the old math you would be cutting a 3⅞" square. Ugh!

For every quarter-square triangle patch you make, add 1½" to the finished size. Example: A 3" finished square plus 1½" seam allowance equals 4½", a very easy round number to rotary-cut. Under the old math you would add 1¼" to the finished size of the square. I have increased this number so that I could sew both types of triangle patches with the ³/₈" seam allowance. You will realize the benefits of the increased size of the quarter-square triangle in the flying geese method.

NOTES FROM NANCY

I totally embrace Cindy's suggestion to skip the ⅛" measurement. Why didn't someone think of that earlier! Before stitching, check the measurement between the needle and the edge of the foot. It might be necessary to move the needle position. Or, consider purchasing a "Little Foot"—the left side of the foot measures a scant ³/₈", which is the perfect width for this technique.

QUARTER-SQUARE TRIANGLES

3 Sew across the square with a ⅜" seam allowance. If you have multiple patches to sew, chain-sew one set of squares after another, thread-pinning in between patches. Turn the chain of squares around and sew ⅜" away from the opposite side of each drawn line. Cut the sections apart.

4 Cut each square on the drawn line to make two half-square triangle blocks.

5 Press each square open with the seam allowances toward the darker fabric. You now have a set of perfect half-square triangle blocks! In any patchwork pattern that contains a half-square triangle or a quarter-square triangle, use my math and reduce the cutting time by half.

6 Trim the corners from the ends of each of the half-square triangle blocks. Once you make the half-square triangle blocks, combine them to create the quarter-square triangle blocks.

7 Layer the two pairs of half-square triangles right sides together with the dark triangles on opposite sides. Fold down the top square to make sure the intersecting seams are aligned. Mark a diagonal line across the seam from corner to corner just like you did in the half-square triangle method.

→

8 Position the two squares so the needle is ⅜" from the drawn line. Use the point of the seam ripper to hold the intersecting seam in place. Sew a ⅜" seam allowance on both sides of the drawn line.

9 Cut the sewn patch in half along the drawn line. Press the seam allowance to one side, or press this final seam open so the patch will lay flatter. You now have two completed quarter-square triangle blocks.

Aligning a Diamond Square

Sewing a triangle onto a square should be easy, right? But how do you know where to place the triangle on the square when the ends are hanging off the edge? Here's a sew simple solution to use anytime you need to add a triangle to a square.

1 Fold the square into quarters. Press the creases on the outside edges of the square.

2 Place the triangle right sides together with the square and align the point of the triangle with the crease line in the square. Sew across the triangle from edge to edge. Press the seams away from the square.

Making a Nine-Patch Block

Instead of cutting individual patches and sewing them together, it's much easier to assemble a nine-patch block by creating some simple strip sets. You can use this method anytime you have several nine-patch blocks to make. Add a ½" seam allowance to the size of the finished square and you have the width of the strips to cut. Sew simple.

3 Sew your first two sections together.

1 Sew three strips together to create each required panel. Panels must be sewn with a scant ¼" seam allowance. Place two of your panels right sides together.

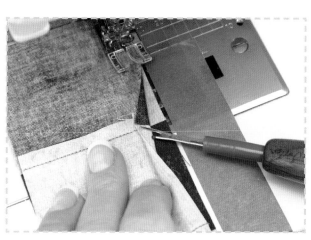

4 As you sew, make sure the strips match at the intersections.

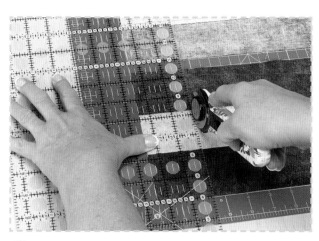

2 Cut across the panels at 2" intervals. Do not separate the strips from each other after cutting. They are ready to be chain-fed through the sewing machine.

5 Add the third section to complete the nine-patch block.

Squaring Up Blocks

Sometimes it's advantageous to create a block from a strip, thereby eliminating the extra step of sewing on a triangle to achieve a corner (such as in the *Garden Connection* pattern). So we simply square up the block to the finished size we need.

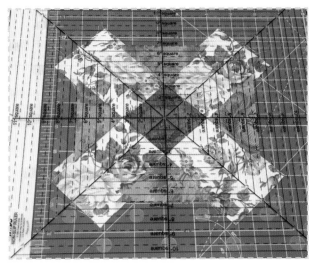

1 Center a square ruler over the block so you can see if it's the same on all four sides. Keep in mind that you have ¼" seams on the outside edge of the block that you must take into consideration. You can only trim where there is enough excess fabric to still allow for the ¼" joining seam allowance.

2 Mark the block where you plan to cut it. Then take it out from under the ruler and follow the marked cutting line.

3 Align the rotary ruler with the marks and trim the block to size.

Quick-Turn Appliqué Method

This is an easy technique of turning under the raw edges on a simple appliqué shape. This method is best suited for large pieces with gentle curves. The use of Do Sew tracing material simplifies the process.

1 Trace the appliqué template on the paper side of freezer paper and cut out. Place your Do Sew right sides together with the fabric. Iron the templates to the right side of the Do Sew.

2 Stitch around the outside edges of the freezer paper template. Remove the freezer paper.

3 Trim the seam allowance to an ⅛" or less.

4 Notch into any deep curves. If you have a spray bottle, spritz lightly on top of the Do Sew before turning. Cut a small hole into the Do Sew. Turn the appliqué right side out and press with a steam iron. The Do Sew should roll under to the wrong side of the fabric.

3-D Appliqué Method

This method of creating three-dimensional appliqués is sew simple with the use of some basic products that you already have on hand.

3 Cut the Steam-A-Seam 2 Lite and fabric together along the traced lines of the freezer paper template.

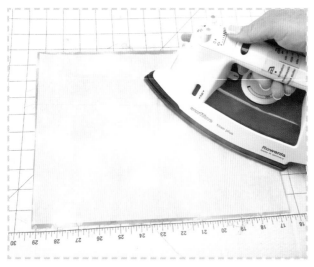

1 Remove one sheet of the release paper from the Steam-A-Seam 2 Lite fusible web. Set this release paper aside to be used later. Place the web on the wrong side of the appliqué fabric. Steam press in place.

4 Peel off the remaining release paper (leaving the web on the fabric) and place the appliqué on the reserved sheet of release paper. Note: The release paper works just like a Teflon pressing sheet.

2 Flip the fabric over and put the freezer paper template on the right side of the fabric. Press in place to hold.

5 Arrange appliqués on top of the release paper, overlapping them as desired. Once satisfied with the arrangement, you can press for five seconds to join appliqués together. This is especially helpful when you have several small pieces that you want to join into a larger unit, such as in *Garden Star*. Note: You can store any of the appliqués on this release paper until you're ready to arrange them on your background fabric.

6 Now that the appliqués have been combined into a larger appliqué unit, you can peel them off the release paper.

7 Using the steam press setting on the iron, press the appliqué unit to the background square.

8 Flip the background square over to the wrong side. Lay a piece of cotton batting on the background fabric. The batting is used to stabilize the stitching and provide the 3-D effects on the appliqué.

9 Select a zigzag stitch or any decorative stitch you like to accent your leaves, flowers or stems. I usually choose different stitches for the stems and the leaves or flowers.

10 Once you complete the decorative stitching, flip the block over and trim the excess batting around the appliqué. This trimming method will create a raised effect once the quilt is layered with batting and backing and the quilting around the appliqué is completed.

Flying Geese

Flying geese units are needed in many patterns. A unit is always twice as wide as it is high. A typical unit finishes 2" × 4". Why make just one flying goose unit when you can make four at a time? This method combines both half-square and quarter-square triangles into one unit.

3 Cut apart on the center drawn line. This gives you two units that look like a jet plane. Press the seams toward the smaller squares.

1 Cut one square the finished width (the bigger measurement) of the desired geese unit plus 1½". This is the large square. Cut four squares the finished height of the desired geese unit plus 1". These are the smaller squares. Place two of the smaller squares right sides together in opposite corners of the larger square. Draw a light pencil line diagonally across the two smaller squares. Notice that the two small squares overlap in the center of the block.

4 Place a remaining small square right sides together on each of the jet planes. Draw a diagonal line on the wrong side of the smaller squares. Stitch ⅜" on both sides of the drawn line.

2 Stitch a ⅜" seam allowance on both sides of the drawn line. Use the point of your seam ripper to guide the squares under the presser foot. Note: Little Foot makes a presser foot with ⅜" on one side and ¼" on the opposite side. This is the foot shown in the photo.

5 Cut the two units apart on the drawn line. Voila! You have four flying geese units.

Folded Triangle Inset Border

This is a fun way to add a little pizzazz to borders on your quilt. The added texture and colors from the folded triangles give another layer of dimension to your finished quilt.

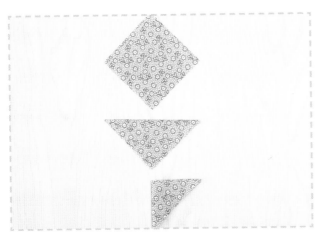

1 Fold your squares in half to form a triangle. Press in half again for a smaller triangle. Press all of the triangles to help hold the creases in place. The number of triangles needed is determined by the length of the border. See the pattern for the specific number and size of triangles to cut.

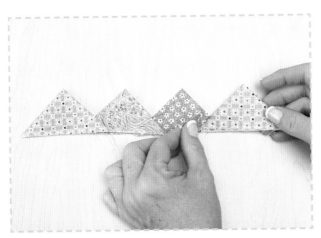

2 Start placing the triangles down in a row long enough to fit on the long side of the border strips. Open the ends of each folded triangle and insert the tip of the next triangle.

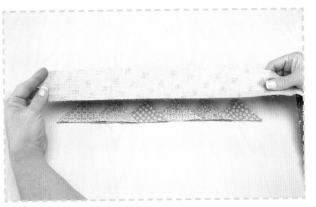

3 Place the border strip right sides together on top of the folded triangles about ¼" from the bottom edge of the triangle row. Securely pin the triangles to the border.

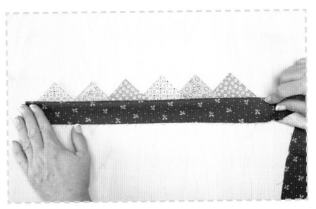

4 Flip the pinned border and triangles over so the border strip is now on the bottom and the triangles are on top. Stitch a scant ¼" from the bottom edge of the triangle row. Press the border strip away from the triangles.

Don't forget to watch the DVD, which is bound into the back of this book, to watch Cindy demonstrate many of her clever techniques.

NOTES FROM **NANCY**

Double Fold Binding

Double fold binding makes a secure and sturdy edge on any quilt.

1 Here is how to join 2¾" × 42" long strips with diagonal seams. Place two short ends right sides together perpendicular to each other. Extend the ends of each strip above and beyond each other so you can see the strip underneath. Place a ruler across the strips and mark the diagonal stitching line with a light pencil or chalk wheel.

2 Stitch on the line. Continue to add strips to the end until you have enough to make one long continuous binding.

3 Trim the excess seam allowance to a ⅜" seam. Press the seams open.

4 Fold the binding in half wrong sides together and press to hold the crease. Wrap the binding around cardboard to keep it from twisting.

5 Starting from the back of the quilt on one side, align the raw edges of the binding strip with the raw edges of the quilt. Leave a 10" unattached strip of binding at the beginning of the stitching. Stitch the binding ⅜" away from the edge. Using a walking foot will keep the binding from shifting.

6 Stop stitching about 3" from the corner of the quilt. Leave the needle down. Fold the binding strip at a 45-degree angle to the right side of the quilt. The 45-degree fold will meet the corner of the quilt.

8 Refold the binding strip back into the 45-degree angle.

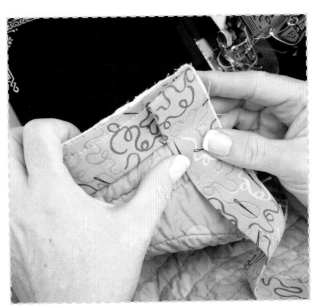

7 Unfold to reveal the crease line. Mark the crease line with a pencil. Sew up to the marked crease line and stop. Backstitch out of the crease line. Cut threads and take the quilt out from under the presser foot.

9 Fold the strip back down onto the adjacent edge of the quilt. Keep the fold of the strip exactly even along the upper edge of the quilt, in line with the raw edge of the side you just stitched.

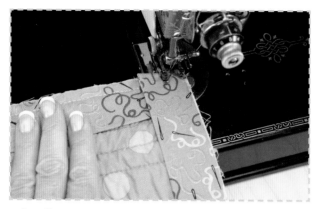

10 Begin sewing from the edge of the fold and continue along the second side of the quilt. Sew all four corners the same way. On the last side, stop sewing about 10" away from where you started sewing.

11 Overlap the last strip across the first unattached binding strip. Measure the overlap to be exactly 2¾". Place a pin to hold the mark. Cut the top strip at the 2¾" mark.

12 Place the ends of the binding strips right sides together, perpendicular to each other. Mark the stitching line with a ruler and chalk wheel.

13 Stitch across the two ends of binding from corner to corner on the diagonal line.

14 Lay the binding back against the raw edge of the quilt to see the fit. Trim the seam and press open. Stitch the rest of the binding to the quilt.

15 Press the binding over from the back of the quilt to the front of the quilt. Flip the quilt to the front side. Form the mitered corners by folding each corner at a 45-degree angle. Press the fold to make a crease.

16 Working from the front of the quilt, place Steam-A-Seam fusible tape (¼" wide) on the edge of the quilt and fuse into place with the iron on the steam setting.

17 Let the paper cool down at least 5 minutes. Carefully pull up the paper tape to reveal the fusible underneath.

18 Set the iron on the steam setting. Press the binding to the quilt, covering up the fusible tape and anchoring the binding to the quilt. Now there is no need to use any clips or pins to hold the binding in place.

19 Stitch down the binding with a blind hem stitch or a decorative stitch. You can reverse the process and start from the front of the quilt and fold the binding to the back. If you stitch in the ditch from the front of the quilt you can catch the edge of the binding on the back, as long as you adhere the binding down with fusible tape first. The wrap around is going to be ⅛" larger providing you stick with the ⅜" seam allowance. I prefer the back-to-front method so I can see the stitching on the front of the quilt.

To keep bindings neatly pressed, roll the pressed fabric around paper towel tubes or small cardboard pieces. I often create the binding and don't sew it to the quilt until a day or two later. This storage technique not only keeps the binding pressed until the next sewing time, but it also keeps the yardage organized.

NOTES FROM **NANCY**

 2

quilts from strips

Nothing is as much fun or as easy as making a quilt from strips. It's amazing what you can do with a combination of strips or shapes cut from a simple strip. In this chapter you will discover four completely different patterns that are all created from strips. The *Trip to Amish Country* quilt combines the old favorite design of Sunshine and Shadow with the Roman Stripe block resulting in one very unique quilt. I really enjoyed going through my stash to find all the beautiful blendable colors for the Sunshine and Shadow section of the quilt to coordinate with my solid fabrics in the Roman Stripe blocks.

The *Hidden Stars* quilt is a simple design with only one shape and yet the way you twist and turn the block creates the stars in the pattern. This quilt is also a great stash buster that combines many colors and fabrics.

The *Puzzle Cube* is similar to a log cabin quilt in the method of assembly because you build the block from the center out The difference is the triangles. The folded squares in the corners appear to be sewn-in triangles; however, the puzzle will be solved once you turn the pages to the pattern.

Finally, the last quilt in this chapter, *Garden Connection,* is quite a chameleon. Its look can be changed so easily with how you use your splash fabric. If you have ever wanted to make a wedding ring quilt but have never taken up the challenge, you might prefer to make this simple strip version. It appears to have circular rings when in fact they are just straight strips. I have included completely different versions of this same simple pattern for you to choose from. My version has the large floral splash fabric as the background of the quilt. My friend Peggy Linnen made this quilt with the large floral splash fabric as the rings in the quilt.

Trip to Amish Country

Pieced by: *Cindy Casciato*

Quilted by: *Eva Birch*

Quilt Sizes:
Double: 72" × 84"
Queen: 85" × 97" (shown)

Look through a roadside quilt shop and you are sure to discover the most popular of quilt patterns: Sunshine and Shadow, also known as Trip Around the World. You might also find the pattern Amish Stripe, also known as the Roman Stripe. Amish Stripe is almost always made with solid colors. *Trip to Amish Country* recognizes the Amish community and celebrates the excellence that the culture brings to the art of quilting.

Pull out your stash fabrics and take a journey down a country lane where buggies and bonnets are commonplace. This quilt provides a great opportunity to explore color and value. There are twelve stash fabrics in these quilts. I used the solids (fabrics A–F) for the Amish Stripe blocks and pulled coordinating blendable prints (fabrics 1–8) for the Trip fabrics. I included two splash prints as my zingers for the Trip quilt. The rest of the splash is added in the borders with three additional fabrics.

YARDAGE

FABRIC	DOUBLE	QUEEN	FOR
Splash: Black fabric (A)	1²⁄₃ yds.	1²⁄₃ yds.	Amish Stripes
Stash: Red-purple fabric (B)	½ yd.	½ yd.	Amish Stripes
Stash: Purple fabric (C)	½ yd.	½ yd.	Amish Stripes
Stash: Turquoise fabric (D)	½ yd.	½ yd.	Amish Stripes
Stash: Bright aqua fabric (E)	½ yd.	½ yd.	Amish Stripes
Stash: Light aqua fabric (F)	½ yd.	½ yd.	Amish Stripes
Stash: Dark purple fabric (1)	½ yd.	⅝ yd.	Trip Around the World
Stash: Blue-purple fabric (2)	½ yd.	⅝ yd.	Trip Around the World
Splash: Print fabric (3)	½ yd.	⅝ yd.	Trip Around the World
Stash: Red-purple fabric (4)	½ yd.	⅝ yd.	Trip Around the World
Stash: Dark teal fabric (5)	½ yd.	⅝ yd.	Trip Around the World
Stash: Medium turquoise fabric (6)	½ yd.	⅝ yd.	Trip Around the World
Stash: Bright aqua fabric (7)	½ yd.	⅝ yd.	Trip Around the World
Stash: Light aqua fabric (8)	½ yd.	⅝ yd.	Trip Around the World
Splash	½ yd.	½ yd.	1st Border
Splash	⅝ yd.	⅝ yd.	2nd Border
Splash	2½ yds.	3 yds.	3rd Border
Binding	1 yd.	1 yd.	Binding
Backing	6 yds. of 40" wide	8 yds. of 40" wide	

CUTS

FABRIC	DOUBLE	QUEEN
Fabric A	Cut eight strips approx. 6" × 42". (Cut these strips after you piece the strip units together. Measure across the strip panel for exact width.) Cut four spacers 2½" × 8". Cut two spacers 1" × 8".	Cut eight strips approx. 6" × 42". (Cut these strips after you piece the strip units together. Measure across the strip panel for exact width.) Cut four spacers 2½" × 8". Cut two spacers 1" × 8".
Fabric B	Cut eight strips 1¾" × 42".	Cut eight strips 1¾" × 42".
Fabric C	Cut eight strips 1½" × 42".	Cut eight strips 1½" × 42".
Fabric D	Cut eight strips 1½" × 42".	Cut eight strips 1½" × 42".
Fabric E	Cut eight strips 1½" × 42".	Cut eight strips 1½" × 42".
Fabric F	Cut eight strips 1¾" × 42".	Cut eight strips 1¾" × 42".
Fabric 1	Cut five strips 2½" × 42".	Cut seven strips 2½" × 42".
Fabric 2	Cut five strips 2½" × 42".	Cut seven strips 2½" × 42".
Fabric 3	Cut five strips 2½" × 42".	Cut seven strips 2½" × 42".
Fabric 4	Cut five strips 2½" × 42".	Cut seven strips 2½" × 42".
Fabric 5	Cut five strips 2½" × 42".	Cut seven strips 2½" × 42".
Fabric 6	Cut five strips 2½" × 42".	Cut seven strips 2½" × 42".
Fabric 7	Cut five strips 2½" × 42".	Cut seven strips 2½" × 42".
Fabric 8	Cut five strips 2½" × 42".	Cut seven strips 2½" × 42".
1st Border	Cut eight strips 2" × 42" crosswise.	Cut eight strips 2" × 42" crosswise.
2nd Border	Cut eight strips 2½" × 42" crosswise.	Cut eight strips 2½" × 42" crosswise.
3rd Border	Cut four strips 8½" × 42" crosswise. Cut four strips 8½" × 54" lengthwise from remaining fabric.	Cut four strips 8½" × 42" crosswise. Cut four strips 8½" × 63" lengthwise from remaining fabric.
Binding	Cut ten strips 2¾" × 42".	Cut eleven strips 2¾" × 42".

MAKE THE AMISH STRIPE BLOCKS

1 Begin laying out the fabrics for the Amish Stripe blocks. First, choose the fabric you want to be the dominant color in the quilt. Place this fabric in the bottom position F as shown in Figure 1. Arrange the other fabrics into positions B–E.

2 Place the B strips right side up with the first strip under your presser foot. Place the C strips right side down lengthwise on top of the B strips. Chain-sew all the B and C strips together.

3 Open up the B/C strips. Place your D strips right sides together lengthwise with the B/C panels and chain-stitch all the D strips to the C strips. Cut the sets apart at the threads.

4 Add strips E and F to the panel in the same manner. Press the seams in one direction. Press one strip at a time from the back, and then the front. Watch for pleats. Make eight pieced bands for either quilt.

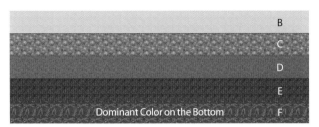

Figure 1

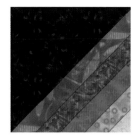

Figure 3

5 Measure across a band from the wrong side. It should be close to 6" wide. This measurement is the width to cut the black fabric A strips.

6 Place a fabric A strip right sides together with a pieced band. Pin together to hold in place and prevent stretching or distorting. Stitch a ¼" seam allowance on both long sides of the band to form a tube. Stitch all the strip bands and fabric A strips together. Press the seams flat to prepare for cutting.

7 Lay the tube on your cutting mat with the fabric A side up. On the reverse side, the dominant strip (G) of the pieced band should be in the bottom position. Place the 45-degree line of the 6" × 24" ruler on the straight top edge of the A strip. Slide the ruler along until the edge of the ruler is at the bottom left corner. Cut along the edge of the ruler with a rotary cutter.

8 Flip the ruler over. Match the 45-degree line with the top straight edge and the tip of the strip where the first triangle was cut. Cut a second triangle. Continue across the A strip, flipping the ruler over and matching the 45-degree line with the straight edge and the tip, and cutting. Each strip yields five blocks—three the same (Figure 3) and two reversed. I chose to use all twenty-four of the same block for the quilt shown. There are sixteen reversed squares leftover that could make another small quilt.

9 Open the stitching at the tip of each block. Press the seam toward the A triangle. You need twenty-four blocks for either quilt (Figure 3). If blocks are larger than 8", trim them to 8" being careful to trim so the diagonal seam touches both corners.

MAKE THE TRIP AROUND THE WORLD CENTER

1 The center of the quilt is constructed of segments cut from pieced bands. Each band consists of sixteen strips, and each of the eight colors (fabrics 1–8) is repeated twice. For the double quilt, cut one of each color strip in half.

2 Following the directions for joining strips in the Amish Stripe blocks, join eight strips (one of each fabric 1–8) into a pieced band. Repeat to make four identical bands plus two short bands (using the half strips) for the double quilt. Make seven identical bands for the queen quilt. The queen quilt needs more for the outer pieced border. Do not press bands yet.

3 Join two pieced bands long edge to long edge, sewing fabric 1 of one band to fabric 8 of a second band. Repeat to make pairs of all bands. Join the two short bands. Each band has a total of sixteen strips with eight fabrics repeated twice.

4 Press the seams of every other strip toward the inside on both sides of the strip. Press the seams of the alternating strips away from them so that the seams will butt up against each other when segments are joined. This is vital for the next sewing step.

5 Fold each panel into a tube by bringing the two long edge strips right sides together. Stitch in a ¼" seam along this joined edge. Trim one short end perpendicular to the rows of stitching to get a straight edge.

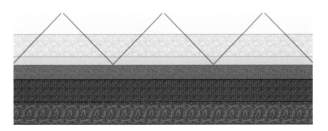

Figure 2

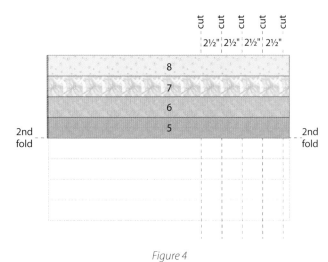

Figure 4

6 Fold each tube in half so that the tube is just four strips high (Figure 4). Cut the tubes in 2½" wide segments. You should get sixteen segments per panel. You need a total of thirty-five segments for either quilt center. You will cut segments for the queen quilt pieced borders later.

7 The quilt center is made in two halves, one for the top and one for the bottom. These halves are joined with a center strip. Figure 7 shows you the fabric numbers from top to bottom of the halves. You will make two identical panels.

8 Take one tube segment and open the seam between fabrics 1 and 8 with your seam ripper. You want to start your panel with fabric 1 at the top. This segment is the middle of the top panel and identical strips will be added to each side. Notice that each segment in the panel is only eleven squares long. You will be removing the bottom five squares in each segment once you have arranged the segments in order.

9 Take a second tube segment and arrange it alongside the first segment so it lines up identically. Shift the second segment down one square, and open the loop between the new top square and what will be the bottom square (between fabrics 7 and 8). The fabric that was the top of the first strip segment is now the bottom of the second. Repeat for the other side of the center (Figure 5). Keep the segments in place, but do not sew them yet.

10 Take another tube segment and arrange it next to the last segment. Shift it down two squares. Open the seam between fabrics 6 and 7. Repeat for the other side. Continue this process until you have eight strips to the left of the center segment and eight to the right of it. Once you are satisfied that all the segments are aligned correctly, count down eleven squares from the top of each segment and remove the bottom five squares from each. This makes the top half of the quilt.

11 Stitch the segments together with a ¼" seam. Press seam allowances away from the center strip. Repeat the steps to make an identical second panel.

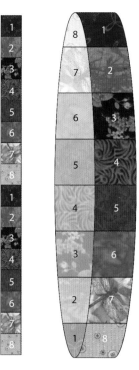

Figure 5

Figure 6

center joining strip

Figure 7

12 You need to create the center horizontal joining strip in the middle of the two panels. The center strip is a combination of two strip segments. Follow the number order on Figure 7 and un-sew the strip loops where necessary. Join them where the diagram indicates. There is an extra 2½" fabric 4 square in the very middle of the strip. Sew that in place.

13 Sew the top and bottom panels to the center strip, staggering seam allowances as you go (Figure 6).

ADD THE AMISH STRIPE BLOCKS

1 Measure your Trip Around the World quilt top through the center for width and length. The ideal measurement is 34½" × 46½". However, please don't despair if your top is a different measurement. Adjustments can be made in the borders.

2 Make two identical rows with six Amish Stripe blocks in each row for the sides of the quilt (Figure 8), noting the orientation of each block. Pin a border to the quilt lengthwise to check for fit. If it is too long, take slightly larger seams between blocks 1 and 2 and between blocks 5 and 6. If the border is too short by more than 1", add spacers as needed. Measure how much it's too short, and divide that number by two. Add ½" to that measurement for seam allowances. Cut two spacers from black fabric (A) that width and 8" long. Un-sew the seam between blocks 1 and 2, and between blocks 5 and 6. Sew a spacer between the blocks. Repeat with the other side border. Sew the borders to the sides of the quilt.

3 Arrange six Amish Stripe blocks in a row. These rows will probably be too short to fit the quilt. To compensate for this, sew a 3" × 8" spacer between blocks 2 and 3, and between blocks 4 and 5. Sew all of the blocks together (Figure 9). Pin the border to the top of the quilt to check for fit. If it is too long, un-sew a seam at each spacer, trim the spacer a bit to make it narrower, and re-sew. Once the borders fit, sew to the top and bottom of the quilt.

Figure 8

← spacer strips →

Figure 9

Figure 12

Figure 10

Figure 11

ADD THE BORDERS

Trip Around the World Border (Queen quilt only)

1 Use the remaining pieced segments from the tubes to create any border design that you want. See Figures 10 and 11 for design ideas, or Figure 12 for final border designs. You need segments that are three squares long. Un-sew the segments as needed.

2 Each border is made with thirty-one segments. Once sewn, lay a side border lengthwise on the quilt to check for length. If it's too long, make adjustments by taking slightly wider seam allowances between segments evenly across the border. Sew the borders to the sides.

3 Sew the top and bottom border in the same way.

Remaining Borders (Both quilts)

1 For the first and second borders, join the crosswise strips in pairs with a diagonal seam. Use a short stitch (15 stitches per inch). Press the seams open. You should have four border strips.

2 For the third border, join the crosswise strips in pairs with a diagonal seam. Join the lengthwise strips in pairs with a diagonal seam. Use a short stitch. Press the seam open.

3 Make four long border sets by combining the first, second and third borders into a strip panel (Figure 13). Press all seams toward the third border.

4 Divide each of the border sets in half and mark the center with a pin.

Figure 13

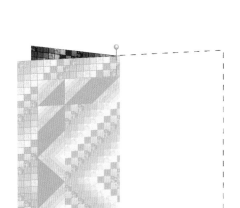

Figure 14

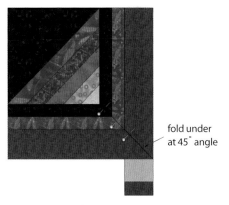

fold under
at 45° angle

Figure 15

5 Divide the quilt in half, both lengthwise and widthwise, and mark with a pin (Figure 14).

6 Starting with the top of the quilt, match one of the border pins with the quilt pin. Pin the border in place.

7 Stitch the border onto the quilt from the center out. Use a ¼" seam allowance. Stop sewing ¼" from each corner. Repeat steps 6–7 for the bottom border.

8 Press both borders away from the quilt. Flip the quilt to the wrong side and pin the side borders in place.

9 Stitch the side borders onto the quilt from the center out. Use a ¼" seam allowance. Stop sewing ¼" from each corner.

10 Press both side borders away from the quilt.

11 Starting with the top border, overlap the end of the top border strip on top of the side borders. Fold the top border strip back at a 45-degree angle, being careful to align each strip with its matching strip on the corresponding side border (Figure 15). Press in place to create a crease/stitching line.

12 Cut two strips of ¼" fusible tape and place one under the top mitered fold at each end of the top border. Press in place.

Figure 16

13 Fold open the border strip and pin a miter in place. Stitch on the creased line. Open the miter to make sure you have matched each of the borders. Trim the excess border strips with a ½" seam allowance. Press to one side. Repeat steps 11–13 for the bottom border. See Figure 16 for the finished layout of the double quilt and the project photo on page 33 for the queen quilt.

QUILT AND BIND

Hidden Stars

Pieced by: *Cindy Casciato*

Quilted by: *Cindy Casciato*

Quilt Sizes:
Wall: 59" × 59" (shown)
Lap: 59" × 74"
Queen: 93" × 108"

Block Size: *15"*

Only one pattern piece makes up this block, but don't let the simplicity of the design fence you in. You'll discover the hidden stars when all the pieces are placed in alternating upright and stacked rows. This quilt can be compiled of many fabrics from your stash. Keep in mind that the warm colors always appear lighter than the cool colors. Yellow, red, orange, pink, rose, gold and beige will all read much lighter than the cool colors of blue, green and purple. The cool colors are always a darker value than a warm color. When you combine a variety of colors and fabrics in a quilt, the best way to organize them is by their value or, simply put, how dark or light they are. In the wall quilt you notice that the stars are light in value, but in the queen quilt the reverse is true. The queen quilt is a study in neutrals accented by teal. The brown is the darkest value in this quilt. Sort through your stash and select two fabrics/colors for your lights and four fabrics/colors for your darks to make light stars. Reverse the recipe and choose four fabrics/colors for your lights and two fabrics/colors for your darks to make dark stars. Choose the recipe that appeals to you.

YARDAGE

FABRIC	WALL	LAP	QUEEN	FOR
Stash: Two or four printed fabrics (light fabrics for the light star recipe, darks for the dark stars)	¾ yd. of each if two prints; ½ yd. of each if four prints	¾ yd. of each if two prints; ½ yd. of each if four prints	1¾ yds. of each if two prints; 1 yd. of each if four prints	Stars
Stash: Four fabrics (dark for the light stars recipe, light for the dark stars)	¾ yd. each	¾ yd. each	1¾ yds. each	Background
Splash (optional)	½ yd.	⅔ yd.	¾ yd.	1st Border
Splash (optional): This gathered border requires three times as many strips all sewn together and gathered over embroidery floss.	1⅓ yds.	1⅝ yds.	2¼ yds.	Alternate Gathered 1st Border
Splash	1¾ yds.	1¾ yds.	2½ yds.	2nd Border
Backing	3¾ yds.	4 yds.	9⅝ yds.	
Binding	⅝ yd.	¾ yd.	1 yd.	

CUTS

FABRIC	WALL	LAP	QUEEN
Star fabrics	Cut eleven strips 3" × 42"; re-cut strips into seventy-two rectangles 3" × 5½".	Cut fourteen strips 3" × 42"; re-cut strips into ninety-six rectangles 3" × 5½".	Cut thirty-five strips 3" × 42"; re-cut strips into 240 rectangles 3" × 5½".
Background fabrics	Cut twenty-one strips 3" × 42"; re-cut strips into 144 rectangles 3" × 5½".	Cut twenty-eight strips 3" × 42"; re-cut strips into 192 rectangles 3" × 5½".	Cut sixty-nine strips 3" × 42"; re-cut strips into 480 rectangles 3" × 5½".
1st Border (optional)	Cut eight strips 2" × 42" crosswise.	Cut eight strips 2" × 42" crosswise.	Cut ten strips 2½" × 42" crosswise.
Gathered 1st Border (optional)	Cut sixteen strips 2" × 42" crosswise.	Cut twenty strips 2" × 42" crosswise.	Cut thirty strips 2½" × 42" crosswise.
2nd Border	Cut eight strips 6" × 42" crosswise.	Cut eight strips 6" × 42" crosswise.	Cut ten strips 7½" × 42" crosswise.
Binding	Cut seven strips 2¾" × 42" crosswise.	Cut nine strips 2¾" × 42" crosswise.	Cut eleven strips 2¾" × 42" crosswise.

MAKE THE STAR BLOCKS

1 Place a star strip right side up and a background strip right side down on top of it at a ninety-degree angle.

2 Draw a diagonal line on the wrong side of the background strip from the upper left corner across the rectangle to the opposite side where the dark rectangle meets the light rectangle (Figure 1 or 2).

3 Press seam toward the dark strip. Repeat steps 1–3 to make two star/background units for each block needed. Note that for the wall and lap quilts, one star strip is yellow/gold and the other star strip is red/orange. For the queen quilt, one star strip is aqua and the other is brown. In addition, join two light background strips (for the dark star blocks) or two dark background strips (for the light star blocks) in the same manner to make the center background unit for each block.

Figure 1 (Light Star Recipe)   Figure 2 (Dark Star Recipe)

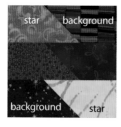

Figure 3 (Light Star Recipe)   Figure 4 (Dark Star Recipe)

Figure 5 (Light Star Recipe)   Figure 6 (Dark Star Recipe)

4 Sew a background unit between two star/background units, turning as needed to make a small block (Figure 3 or 4). Press seam allowances in one direction.

5 Sew small blocks together in groups of four as shown in Figure 5 or 6 to create one large 15" block. For the wall quilt, make a total of thirty-six small blocks. Join them in groups of four to create nine large blocks. For the lap quilt, make a total of forty-eight small blocks. Join them in groups of four to create twelve large blocks. For the queen quilt, make a total of 120 small blocks. Join them in groups of four to create thirty large blocks.

JOIN INTO ROWS

For the wall quilt, sew the nine large blocks together into three horizontal rows. Join the rows. Press the seam allowances in opposing directions.

For the lap quilt, sew the twelve large blocks together into four horizontal rows (Figure 8). Join the rows. Press the seam allowances in opposing directions.

For the queen quilt, sew the thirty large blocks together into six horizontal rows (see Figure 9). Join the rows. Press the seam allowances in opposing directions.

MAKE THE GATHERED BORDER (OPTIONAL)

You will need some crochet cotton thread that comes in a ball with about 300 yards. This border adds an interesting texture to the quilt. See a closeup of it on page 30.

1 For the wall and lap quilts, join four or five strips together with diagonal seams for each side of the quilt. For the queen quilt, join seven strips together with diagonal seams for each side of the quilt. Each border strip should be about three times as long as the side of the quilt.

2 Set up your machine to a wide zigzag stitch that will completely couch over the crochet cotton thread without stitching through it.

3 Lay the crochet thread near the long edge of a border strip leaving a 10" tail of thread at each end. Couch the thread to both long sides of each of the border strips (Figure 7). Pull up the thread at one end of the strip to gather the border. Continue to gather the border strip until you have the border length needed to attach it to the quilt.

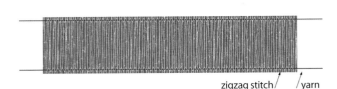

zigzag stitch / / yarn

Figure 7

4 Sew the gathered border right sides together to the quilt. You may need to take up a ⅜" seam allowance to avoid catching the crochet thread in the seams. Sew the remaining gathered borders to the sides, overlapping the top and bottom borders at the corners.

MAKE THE BORDERS (WALL AND LAP QUILTS ONLY)

1 To make the first border (if you're not using the gathered border), join pairs of border strips together with a diagonal seam. Press seams open. Sew the strips to the top and bottom of the quilt. Trim the ends of the strips to fit the quilt. Sew the strips to the sides of the quilt. Trim the ends of the strips to fit the quilt.

2 To make the second border, join pairs of strips together with a diagonal seam. Press all seams open. Sew the strips to the top and bottom of the quilt. Trim the ends of the strips to fit the quilt. Sew the strips to the sides of the quilt. Trim the ends of the strips to fit the quilt. Press all border strips away from the quilt. See project photo on page 40 for the finished layout of the wall quilt (done in the light star recipe). See Figure 8 for the lap quilt (done in the light star recipe).

MAKE THE BORDERS (QUEEN ONLY)

1 To make the first border (if you're not using the gathered border), join pairs of border strips together with a diagonal seam. Press seams open. Sew the strips to the top and bottom of the quilt. Trim the ends of the strips to fit the quilt. Join three strips together with a diagonal seam. Press seams open. Sew the strips to the sides of the quilt. Trim the ends of the strips to fit the quilt.

2 To make the second border, join the pairs of strips together with a diagonal seam. Press seams open. Sew the strips to the top and bottom of the quilt. Trim the ends of the strips to fit the quilt. Join the strips together with a diagonal seam. Press seams open. Sew the strips to the sides

of the quilt. Trim the ends of the strips to fit the quilt. Press all border strips away from the quilt. See Figure 9 for the finished layout of the queen quilt (done in the dark star recipe).

QUILT AND BIND

Figure 8

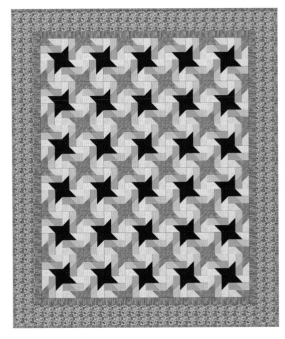

Figure 9

The Puzzle Cube

Pieced by: *Cindy Casciato*

Quilted by: *Cindy Casciato*

Quilt Sizes:
Twin: 58½" × 73" (shown)
Queen: 82½" × 97½"

Block Size: *12½"*

This is a great quilt to use up some stash fabrics in your collection. All of the blocks are comprised of stash fabrics and the splashfabric is used for the borders. You may want to select a family of colors that are closely related (i.e., next to one another on the color wheel. My family of colors include red-purple, purple and blue-purple. Any combination of colors that are next to one another on the color wheel are called analogous. When you combine a lot of fabrics together, you need to find continuity between them. An analogous color recipe pulls the quilt together and provides that continuity.

YARDAGE

FABRIC	TWIN	QUEEN	FOR
Stash: Light (pink) print (A)	1 yd.	1½ yds.	Triangles
Stash: Medium (lavender) print (B)	¼ yd.	½ yd.	Strip Panel Center of Blocks
Stash: Medium (blue-purple) fabric (C)	⅛ yd.	¼ yd.	Strip Panel Center of Blocks
Stash: Medium (purple) print (D)	¾ yd.	1 yd.	Blocks
Stash: Dark (burgundy) print (E)	¾ yd.	1 yd.	Blocks
Stash: Dark (deep plum) print (F)	1 yd.	1¼ yds.	Blocks
Stash: Light fabric	¼ yd.	³⁄₈ yd.	Sashing Squares
Stash: Medium fabric	1 yd.	1¾ yds.	Sashing
Splash: Medium-dark fabric	2 yds.	1 yd.	1st Border
Splash: Dark fabric	N/A	2½ yds.	2nd Border
Binding	⅔ yd.	⅞ yd.	
Backing	4½ yds.	7½ yds. crosswise	

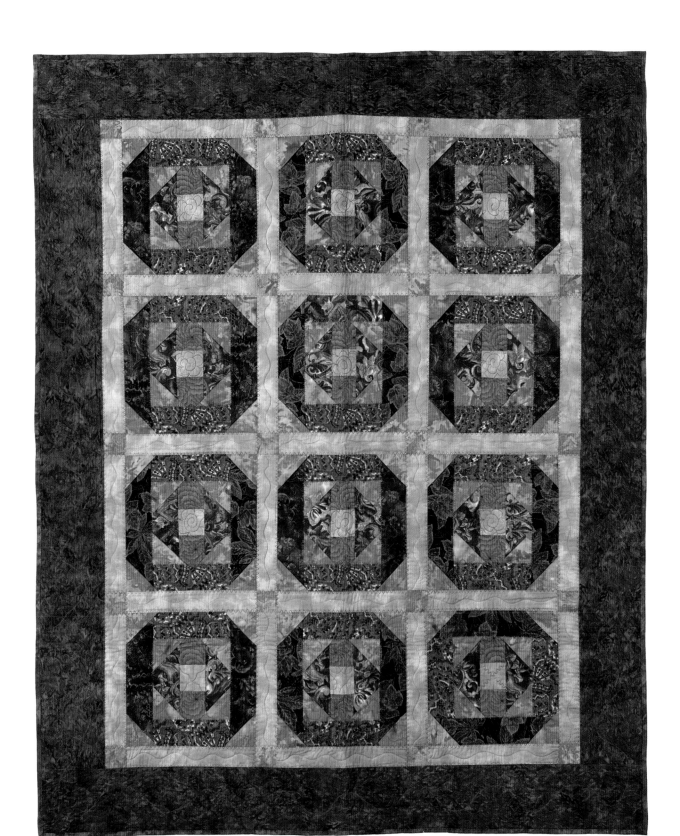

CUTS

FABRIC	TWIN	QUEEN
Fabric A	Cut eight strips 3" × 42"; re-cut strips into ninety-six squares 3".	Cut thirteen strips 3" × 42"; re-cut strips into 160 squares 3".
Fabric B	Cut two strips 3" × 42".	Cut four strips 3" × 42".
Fabric C	Cut one strip 3" × 42".	Cut two strips 3" × 42".
Fabric D	Cut five strips 3" × 42"; re-cut into twenty-four strips 3" × 8".	Cut eight strips 3" × 42"; re-cut into forty strips 3" × 8".
Fabric E	Cut five strips 3" × 42"; re-cut into twenty-four strips 3" × 8".	Cut eight strips 3" × 42"; re-cut into forty strips 3" × 8".
Fabric F	Cut eight strips 3" × 42"; re-cut into twenty-four strips 3" × 13".	Cut fourteen strips 3" × 42"; re-cut into forty strips 3" × 13".
Light sashing fabric	Cut two strips 2½" × 42"; re-cut into twenty squares 2½" × 2½".	Cut three strips 3" × 42"; re-cut into thirty squares 3" × 3".
Medium sashing fabric	Cut eleven strips 2½" × 42"; re-cut into thirty-one strips 2½" × 13".	Cut seventeen strips 3" × 42"; re-cut into forty-nine strips 3" × 13".
1st Border	Cut eight strips 7" × 42" crosswise.	Cut eight strips 3" × 42" crosswise.
2nd Border	N/A	Cut ten strips 8" × 42" crosswise.
Binding	Cut seven strips 2¾" × 42" crosswise.	Cut ten strips 2¾" × 42" crosswise.

MAKE THE BLOCKS

1 Sew together one C strip in between two D strips to create one strip set (Figure 1). Make one strip set for the twin quilt and two for the queen.

2 Re-cut the strip set into 3" segments (Figure 1). Cut twelve segments for the twin quilt and twenty segments for the queen.

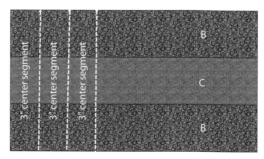

Figure 1

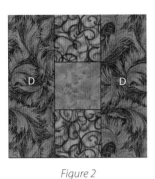

Figure 2

Figure 3

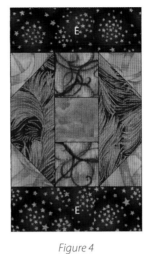

Figure 4

Figure 5

3 Chain-sew D strips on both sides of each center segment (Figure 2). Use the thread-pinning technique. The final piece should measure 8" square.

4 Fold half of the A squares in half on the diagonal, wrong sides together, and pin to each of the four corners (Figure 3).

5 Sew the E strips on the top and bottom of the squares (Figure 4).

6 The last two F strips are sewn on opposing sides of the squares (Figure 5).

7 Fold the remainder of the A squares in half diagonally, wrong sides together. Press to hold.

8 Pin the triangles to the outside corners of the block or machine baste in place. The squares should measure 13" from raw edge to raw edge (Figure 6).

Figure 6

Consider auditioning fabric choices prior to cutting the strips and squares. Cut one 3" crosswise strip from various fabrics in your stash. Lay out the fabrics in a makeshift Puzzle Cube block. Choosing a light fabric color for fabric A and medium to dark fabrics for the other selections will cause the cube element to have visual impact.

NOTES FROM **NANCY**

Rather than choosing a solid strip for the sashing strip, Cindy has cleverly designed the sashing strips to include elements that enhance the quilt design. Often when quilting, I don't pin the strips together, yet this time I do. Be certain to pin the seams of the sashing squares at the corresponding intersection of the blocks. You'll be glad you did!

ASSEMBLE THE QUILT

1 Sew the sashing squares to the ends of the sashing strips. Join the sashing strips together to create the horizontal rows. For the twin quilt, make five horizontal sashing rows with four squares and three sashing strips in each row (Figure 7). For the queen quilt, make six horizontal sashing rows with five squares and four sashing strips in each row (Figure 8).

2 For the twin quilt, make four rows with three blocks and four vertical sashing strips in each row (Figure 9). For the queen quiltk, make five rows with four blocks and five vertical sashing strips in each row (Figure 10).

3 Alternating sashing rows and block rows, join rows together to make the twin quilt (Figure 11) or the queen quilt (Figure 12).

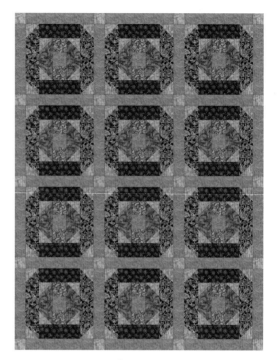

Figure 11

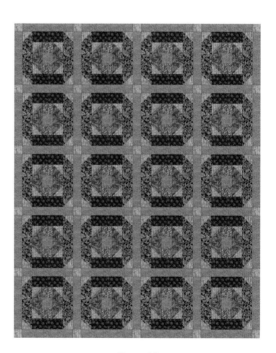

Figure 12

Figure 7

Figure 8

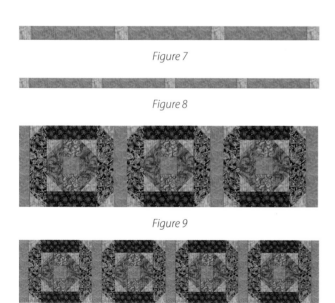

Figure 9

Figure 10

ADD THE BORDERS

1 Join two border strips for each side of the twin quilt. Join two and a half strips for each side of the queen quilt. Pin the first side borders right sides together with the sides of the quilt. Stitch to the quilt and trim the edges of the strip even with the top and bottom of the quilt.

2 Repeat for the top and bottom of the quilt. The border edges will extend over the side borders. Trim edges even with the sides of the quilt. See the project photo on page 45 for the finished layout of the twin quilt.

3 Queen only: Pin the second side borders right sides together with the sides of the quilt and stitch. Repeat for the top and bottom of the quilt. The border edges will extend over the side borders. Trim edges even with the sides of the quilt. See Figure 13 for the finished layout of the queen quilt.

QUILT AND BIND

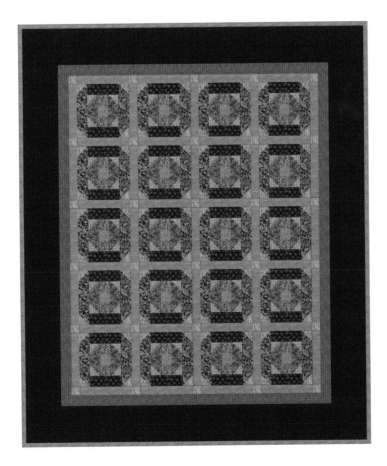

Figure 13

Garden Connection

Pieced by: *Claudia Bissler*

Quilted by: *JoAnne West*

Quilt Sizes:
Twin: 71" × 85" (shown)
King: 99" × 127"

Block Size: *7"*

Have you always loved the wedding ring pattern but knew you didn't want to fussy cut all those individual pieces? You can create a new modern version of this old favorite with assembly line piecing and easy-to-cut strips. Use floral for the strips or put it in the background—both look amazing.

YARDAGE

FABRIC	TWIN	KING	FOR
Splash: Large floral (A)	4 yds.	7 yds.	Background and 1st Border
Stash: 1st Medium print (B)	½ yd.	2½ yds.	Connection Blocks
Stash: 2nd Medium print (C)	1½ yds.	2½ yds.	X Blocks and 3rd Border
Stash: Dark print (D)	1 yd.	2¼ yds.	X and Connection Blocks
Stash: Accent print (E)	¾ yd.	1¼ yds.	X Blocks and 2nd Border
Stash: Binding	¾ yd.	1 yd.	
Backing	5¼ yds.	11¼ yds.	

CUTS

FABRIC	TWIN	KING
Large floral (A)	Cut seven strips 4" × 42" crosswise.	Cut seventeen strips 4" × 42" crosswise.
	Cut three strips 4¾" × 42" crosswise; re-cut strips into twenty squares 4¾"; re-cut squares twice on the diagonal for quarter-square triangles.	Cut six strips 4¾" × 42" crosswise; re-cut strips into forty-eight squares 4¾"; re-cut squares twice on the diagonal for quarter-square triangles.
	Cut three strips 7½" × 42" crosswise; re-cut strips into twelve squares 7½".	Cut seven strips 7½" × 42" crosswise; re-cut strips into thirty-five squares 7½".
	Cut four strips 7½" × 42" crosswise Then cut four strips 7½" × remaining length of fabric.	Cut four strips 7½" × 42" crosswise Then cut four strips 7½" × remaining length of fabric.
1st Medium print (B)	Cut seven strips 2¼" × 42" crosswise.	Cut seventeen strips 2¼" × 42" crosswise.
2nd Medium print (C)	Cut four strips 4½" × 42" crosswise.	Cut eight strips 4½" × 42" crosswise.
	Cut ten strips 3" × 42" crosswise.	Cut fourteen strips 3" × 42" crosswise.
Dark print (D)	Cut seven strips 2¼" × 42" crosswise.	Cut seventeen strips 2¼" × 42" crosswise.
	Cut four strips 4½" × 42"; re-cut into forty rectangles 3" × 4½".	Cut eight strips 4½" × 42"; re-cut into ninety-six rectangles 3" × 4½".
Accent (E)	Cut two strips 3" × 42" crosswise.	Cut four strips 3" × 42" crosswise.
	Cut eight strips 2" × 42" crosswise.	Cut fourteen strips 2" × 42" crosswise.
Binding	Cut eight strips 2¾" × 42" crosswise.	Cut twelve strips 2¾" × 42" crosswise.

Note: Use a small stitch length and press all seams open when making these blocks.

MAKE THE CONNECTION BLOCKS

1 Sew the 2¼" × 42" B and D strips and the 4" × 42" A strips into the Connection block strip set. Make seven strip sets for the twin quilt and seventeen strip sets for the king quilt. Use a scant ¼" seam allowance.

2 Press the seams of the Connection block strip open. The strip set ideally measures 7½" wide after piecing and pressing.

3 Cut across the strip sets every 7½" (Figure 1). Each strip set yields five blocks. For the twin quilt, make thirty-one blocks and eighty-two for the king quilt.

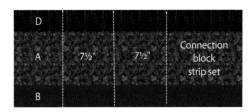

Figure 1

MAKE THE X BLOCKS

1 Sew a strip panel of one 3" × 42" E strip and two 4½" × 42" C strips. Make two strip sets for the twin quilt and four for the king quilt.

2 Press seams to the center strip. Re-cut the strip set into 3" sections (Figure 2). Each strip set yields thirteen strip sections. Cut a total of twenty sections for the twin quilt and forty-eight for the king quilt.

Figure 2

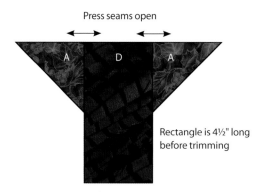

Figure 3

3 Position the short side of a large floral triangle even with one end of a 3" × 4½" dark rectangle. With right sides together, stitch the triangle to the rectangle. Repeat for the opposite side with a second triangle. Press the seam allowances open(Figure 3). Make forty triangle sections for the twin quilt and ninety-six for the king quilt.

4 Make a stack of ten 3" × 42" accent strip sections. Sew a triangle section to one side of each accent strip section. You can pin at the intersections if you like or try my method of using a stiletto or the pointed end of your trusty seam ripper. Chain-piece ten X blocks at a time by feeding the sections under the needle without breaking the threads in between the sections.

5 Turn the sections around and feed the opposite side under the machine and add the other triangle sections (Figure 4). Cut the threads when you complete ten X blocks. Repeat the process until you have twenty X blocks for the twin and forty-eight for the king quilt.

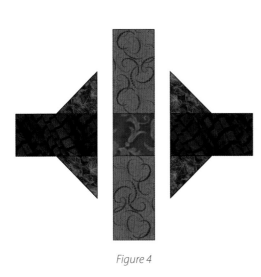

Figure 4

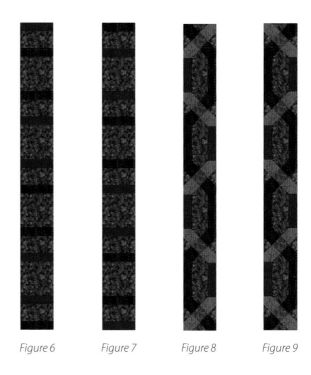

Figure 6   *Figure 7*   *Figure 8*   *Figure 9*

6 Press the final seam allowances for the X block open.

7 Square up the X blocks to 7½" × 7½" (Figure 5).

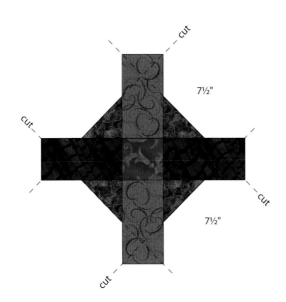

Figure 5

MAKE THE ROWS

Twin Quilt

1 Divide the quilt into seven vertical rows with nine units in each row.

2 Stack two piles of Connection blocks and large floral squares next to your sewing machine. Make two rows that look like Figure 6. Press all the seams toward the Connection blocks.

3 Make one row that looks like Figure 7. Press all the seams toward the Connection blocks.

4 Make two rows that look like Figure 8. Press all the seams toward the Connection blocks.

5 Make two rows that look like Figure 9. Press all the seams toward the Connection blocks.

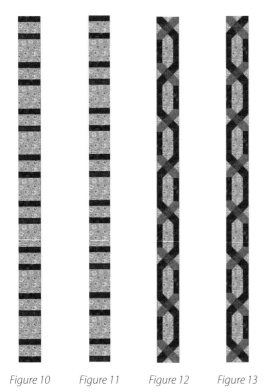

Figure 10   Figure 11   Figure 12   Figure 13

4 Make three rows that look like Figure 12. Press all the seams toward the Connection blocks.

5 Make three rows that look like Figure 13. Press all the seams toward the Connection blocks.

ASSEMBLE THE QUILT TOP AND ADD BORDERS

1 Assemble the quilt top by joining the vertical rows. See the project photo on page 51 for placement in the twin quilt and Figure 14 for the queen quilt. The seam allowances are already pressed in opposing directions to make joining the rows simple. I recommend pinning at the intersections and using a stiletto or the pointed end of your trusty seam ripper to hold the seams in place when you take out the pins to stitch.

2 For the first border, join the 7½" × 42" crosswise strips of large floral fabric in pairs with a diagonal seam. Use a short stitch (15 stitches per inch). Press seams open.

3 Join the lengthwise strips in pairs with a diagonal seam. Use a short stitch (15 stitches per inch). Press seams open.

King Quilt

1 Divide the quilt into eleven vertical rows with fifteen units in each row.

2 Stack two piles of Connection blocks and squares next to your sewing machine. Make three rows that look like Figure 10. Press all the seams toward the Connection blocks.

3 Make two rows that look like Figure 11. Press all the seams toward the Connection blocks.

NOTES FROM **NANCY**

For ease in stitching, position the fabric under the presser foot with the already sewn patch-work seam allowances pressed downward.

Figure 14

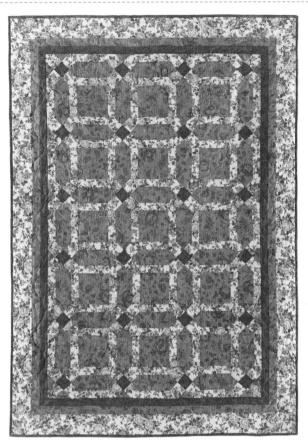

Variation Quilt

4 Sew the crosswise borders on the top and bottom of the quilt. Press the seams toward the border strips. Cut the ends of the strips even with the edges of the quilt.

5 Sew the lengthwise borders on the sides of the quilt. Press the seams toward the border strips. Cut the ends of the strips even with the edges of the quilt.

6 For the second border, join the 2" × 42" crosswise strips of accent fabric in pairs with a diagonal seam for a total of four pairs per quilt. Add one extra strip to two of the pairs for the twin quilt. Add an extra strip to all four pairs for the king quilt. Use a short stitch (15 stitches per inch). Press seams open.

7 Sew the top and bottom borders on the quilt. Press the seams toward the border strips. Cut the ends of the strips even with the edges of the quilt.

8 Sew the side borders on the quilt. Press the seams toward the border strips. Cut the ends of the strips even with the edges of the quilt.

9 For the third border, join the 3" × 42" strips of the second medium fabric in pairs with a diagonal seam. Use a short stitch (15 stitches per inch). Add a third strip to two of the pairs for the king quilt, and join a total of four strips for each side border of the king quilt.

10 Sew the shorter borders to the top and bottom of the quilt. Press the seams toward the border strips. Cut the ends of the strips even with the edges of the quilt.

11 Sew the longer borders to the sides of the quilt. Press the seams toward the border strips. Cut the ends of the strips even with the edges of the quilt. Stay stitch the long side of the final crosswise borders. This will keep them from stretching.

QUILT AND BIND

3

quilts from squares

Now it's time to have fun with squares. Whether you already have some collections of squares in your stash or if you start with fabric cut into squares, these quilts are just fun to make.

Let's get started with the *Fabriholics Fantasy* quilt. If you happen to have a collection of 5" squares on hand, you can start sewing right away. Even if you don't, it won't take long to get into this quilt.

Rescue Me is a unique quilt pattern that can either showcase rescued embroidery squares or your own embroidery. Pearl Bender embroidered the blocks that later became part of this beautiful quilt. Everyone's favorite blocks, the nine-patch and Attic Window, are combined to create a one of a kind quilt design.

If you just want to have fun and make a quilt because it's so cute, you won't be able to resist *Whimsy's Butterflies*. Whimsy, my fantasy cat, is having too much fun in his garden of butterflies. You will also learn an easy quick-turn appliqué method using a neat product called Do Sew.

Fabriholics Fantasy

Pieced by: *Cindy Casciato*
Quilted by: *Cindy Casciato*

Quilt Sizes:
Wall: 49½" × 49½" (shown)
Lap: 49½" × 67½"
Full: 71½" × 89½"

Block Size: *4½"*

This amazing quilt utilizes an abundance of stash fabrics. Both versions of this pattern rely heavily on the principles of value.

Fabric Option One: For the star points, choose a color family on the darker side of the color wheel. Select any of the complementary hues as the mediums. Choose neutrals for the light squares.

Fabric Option Two: Make this quilt faster by choosing one dark splash fabric for the star points, two medium stash fabrics for the accent and one large print splash fabric for the center squares of the star. To keep things interesting, choose two prints for the background. One should be a light, the other a medium to complement the large print splash fabric. Choose either the large print fabric or the star point fabric for the border.

YARDAGE

FABRIC	WALL	LAP	FULL	FOR
Splash: Dark fabric (A)	Two fat quarters	Three fat quarters	Five fat quarters	Quarter-Square Units
Splash: Dark fabric (B)	Two fat quarters	Three fat quarters	Five fat quarters	Quarter-Square Units
Stash: Medium accent (C)	Two fat quarters	Three fat quarters	Five fat quarters	Quarter-Square Units
Stash: Light print (D)	Two fat quarters	Three fat quarters	Five fat quarters	Quarter-Square Units
Stash: Light-medium scraps (E)	¾ yd.	1 yd.	1½ yds.	5" Background Squares
Stash: Medium scraps (F) (optional: choose this or H)	2" strips	2" strips	2" strips	Nine-Patch Blocks
Stash: Light scraps (G) (optional: choose this or H)	2" strips	2" strips	2" strips	Nine-Patch Blocks
Splash: Large print (H) (optional: choose this or F & G)	½ yd.	1¼ yds.	1½ yds.	5" Squares (in place of Nine-Patch Blocks)
Light/medium scraps (optional)	1 yd.	1¼ yds.	1½ yds.	Pieced Border
Splash: Floral fabric (optional)	1 yd.	1¼ yds.	1½ yds.	Plain Border
Binding	⅝ yd.	⅝ yd.	⅞ yd.	
Backing	3⅜ yds.	4¼ yds.	5½ yds.	

CUTS

FABRIC	WALL	LAP	FULL
Dark (A)	Cut ten 6" squares.	Cut fifteen 6" squares.	Cut twenty-eight 6" squares.
Dark (B)	Cut ten 6" squares.	Cut fifteen 6" squares.	Cut twenty-eight 6" squares.
Medium (C)	Cut ten 6" squares.	Cut fifteen 6" squares.	Cut twenty-eight 6" squares.
Light (D)	Cut ten 6" squares.	Cut fifteen 6" squares.	Cut twenty-eight 6" squares.
Light-medium (E)	Cut twenty-five 5" squares.	Cut thirty-five 5" squares.	Cut sixty-three 5" squares.
Medium scraps (F)	See assembly	See assembly	See assembly
Light scraps (G)	See assembly	See assembly	See assembly
Large print (H) (optional: choose this or use F & G)	Cut sixteen 5" squares.	Cut twenty-four 5" squares.	Cut forty-eight 5" squares.
Pieced border (optional)	Cut forty light 5" squares.	Cut forty-eight light 5" squares.	Cut sixty-four light 5" squares.
Floral border (optional)	Cut six strips 5" × 42".	Cut eight strips 5" × 42".	Cut ten strips 5" × 42".
Binding	Cut six strips 2¾" × 42".	Cut seven strips 2¾" × 42".	Cut nine strips 2¾" × 42".

MAKE THE QUARTER-SQUARE UNITS

1. Follow the instructions for making quarter-square triangles in the Techniques section (page 17). Remember to use a ⅜" seam allowance. To make a 4-fabric quarter-square unit like those in these quilts, refer to the directions in *Caribbean Splash* on page 89. Position the dark triangles opposite each other as shown in Figure 1. Use chain-sewing and thread-pinning to speed up the process.

2. Make forty quarter-square units for the wall quilt, fifty-eight units for the lap quilt and 110 units for the full quilt.

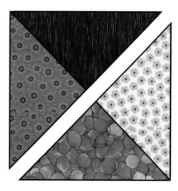

Figure 1

MAKE THE NINE-PATCH BLOCKS (OPTIONAL)

The quilts shown all have nine-patch blocks in the centers of the "stars". However, you can use large-scale print 5" squares in place of the nine-patch blocks. If you prefer plain squares, skip to the next section.

1. Following the instructions for making nine-patch blocks on page 19, sew three of your 2" strips to create each panel. You may use a variety of fabric strips or they could all be the same dark fabric and the same light fabric. Make two panels with a light strip sandwiched between two dark strips. Make one panel with a dark between two lights (Figure 2). All seams must be a scant ¼". Please check for accuracy. These panels will measure 5" across when sewn correctly. Press all seams toward the dark.

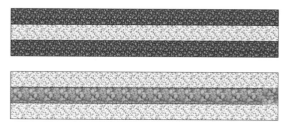

Figure 2

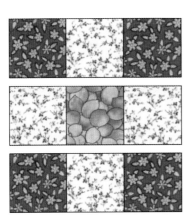

Figure 3

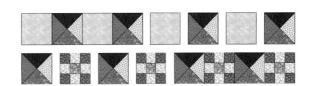

Directional pressing can play an important role when creating a nine-patch block. Press the seams of one panel away from the center and the seams of the companion panel toward the center. When seaming the subcuts, the seams at each intersection will be pressed in opposite directions, making the seaming process a breeze!

NOTES FROM NANCY

2 Place a single light-dark-light panel right sides together with a dark-light-dark panel. Straighten the ends.

3 Cut the stacked panels into 2" wide segments as needed for the number of blocks you are making. Do not separate these strips after cutting. They are ready to be chain-fed through the sewing machine.

4 Recut the remaining dark-light-dark panel into 2" sections.

5 Join three segments to make each block (Figure 3). Make the following: sixteen nine-patch blocks for the wall quilt, twenty-four blocks for the lap quilt, and forty-eight blocks for the full quilt.

ASSEMBLE THE QUILT TOP

Each quilt is made with two kinds of block rows that alternate with one another. Follow the directions for the quilt you are making.

Wall and Lap Quilt

1 For the odd-numbered rows, join five background 5" squares with four quarter-square units. Take note of the orientation of the dark triangles in the quarter-square units. Press the seam allowances toward the plain squares. For the wall quilt, make five rows like this. For the lap quilt, make seven rows like this.

2 For the even-numbered rows, join five quarter-square units with four nine-patch blocks or four large-print 5" squares. Press the seam allowances toward the plain squares or nine-patch blocks. For the wall quilt, make four rows like this. For the lap quilt, make six rows like this.

3 Join the rows, alternating types. Press the seam allowances between rows in one direction. See Figure 5 for the wall quilt and Figure 6 for the lap quilt

Figure 4

Figure 5

Figure 6

Full Quilt

1 For the odd-numbered rows, join seven background 5" squares with six quarter-square units. Take note of the orientation of the dark triangles in the quarter-square units. Press the seam allowances toward the plain squares. Make nine rows like this.

2 For the even-numbered rows, join seven quarter-square units with six nine-patch blocks or four large-print 5" squares. Press the seam allowances toward the plain squares or nine-patch blocks. Make eight rows like this.

3 Join the rows, alternating types. Press the seam allowances between rows in one direction.

ADD THE BORDERS

Choose either the pieced border made with 5" light squares (shown on page 69) to use more of your stash fabric, or select a splash fabric to make a border that finishes 4½" for either the wall or lap quilt. The full quilt has either a small inner border that finishes 2" and a plain outer border that finishes 4½", or a pieced border like the wall quilt.

Wall Quilt (pieced border)

1 For the wall quilt, join nine light 5" squares to make each side border. Audition the border along the side of the quilt to see if it fits. If it is too long, take slightly large seams between blocks until it fits. Sew to the sides.

2 For the wall quilt, join eleven light 5" squares to make the top border. Audition the border for fit and adjust length as needed. Sew to the top. Repeat for the bottom.

Note: In the wall quilt shown on page 59, four of the 5" squares are replaced with nine-patch blocks. If you prefer this, make four more nine-patch blocks and substitute them for four of the 5" squares.

Lap Quilt (pieced border)

For the lap quilt, repeat steps 1 and 2 above, joining thirteen 5" squares for each side border and eleven squares for the top and bottom borders. Sew the side borders to the quilt first.

Full Quilt (pieced border)

Note: This version does not include the 2" plain border.

For the full quilt, repeat steps 1 and 2 above for the wall quilt, joining seventeen 5" squares for each side border and fifteen squares for the top and bottom borders. Sew the side borders to the quilt first.

All Quilts (plain border)

1 The plain border is made with 5" × 42" strips. For the wall quilt, cut two strips in half and join 1½" strips for each side. For the lap quilt, join strips in pairs with a diagonal seam. Use a short stitch (15 stitches per side). Press the seams open.

2 Sew the borders to the sides of the quilt first. Cut the ends of the strips even with the edges of the quilt. Sew the borders to the top and bottom and trim.

3 The full quilt in Figure 7 has an additional narrow inner border (optional). If you wish to add this, cut eight strips of a splash fabric 2½" × 42". Join strips in pairs. Sew a border to each side. Trim the ends even with the quilt. Sew borders to the top and bottom and trim.

4 For the outer border on the full quilt, join four of the 5" border strips in pairs, and join remaining strips in two groups of three strips. Sew a long border to each side. Trim the ends even with the quilt. Sew the shorter borders to the top and bottom and trim.

QUILT AND BIND

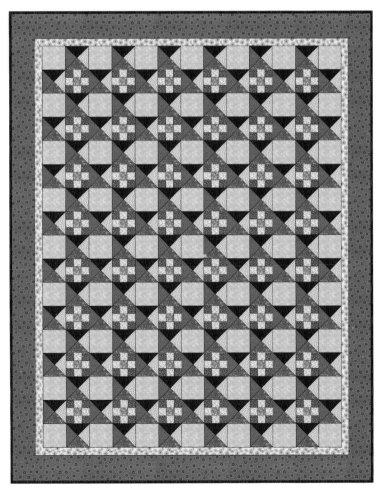

Figure 7

Rescue Me

Pieced by: *Cindy Casciato*

Quilted by: *Eva Birch*

Quilt Sizes:
Crib: 40" × 49"
Wall/Lap: 64" × 64" (shown)

Block Size: *9"*

I found the embroidered blocks in this quilt in the bottom of a box of Christmas bulbs at a local church rummage sale. I had no idea what I would do with them at the time but I knew the workmanship was exquisite and I had to have them. Once I decided to put them in this quilt for my new book, I had to solve the mystery of who made the blocks.

My search led me to Sara Maxwell. Sara knew that they were her grandmother Pearl Bender's leftover blocks. Pearl passed away in 2007 at the age of 84 after having made many quilts which were given to her daughters and their children. Pearl's family was so pleased to see their mother's work finished in this quilt, and they brought out several of Pearl's other quilts to show me. Of all the quilts I have made, this one will always have a special place in my heart. I was able to share skills with another quilter of the past and continue her legacy of quilting. The embroidered blocks were from patterns in the *Workbasket* magazine.

Vintage fabrics and rescued blocks are plentiful at any local flea market. Keep in mind that some of these old pieces are stained or worked on very flimsy fabrics. You may need to soak out the stains, if possible, and reinforce the blocks with an underlayer of muslin. In the nine-patch block, I used fabrics that were shades of the same color, or colors that are close together on the color wheel such as blues and purples. See page 8 for more information on choosing colors.

YARDAGE

FABRIC	CRIB	WALL/LAP	FOR
Stash: 1st Dark fabric (A)	¼ yd.	½ yd.	Nine-Patch Blocks
Stash: Medium dark fabric (B)	¼ yd.	½ yd.	Nine-Patch Blocks
Stash: Medium fabric (C)	¼ yd.	½ yd.	Nine-Patch Blocks
Stash: 1st Light fabric (D)	¼ yd.	½ yd.	Nine-Patch Blocks
Stash: Medium light fabric (E)	¼ yd.	½ yd.	Nine-Patch Blocks
Stash: 2nd Light fabric (F)	¼ yd.	½ yd.	Nine-Patch Blocks
Stash: 2nd Dark fabric (G)	¼ yd.	½ yd.	Attic Window Blocks
Stash: 2nd Medium fabric (H)	¼ yd.	½ yd.	Attic Window Blocks
Splash: Rescued squares or other splash fabric (I)	¼ yd.	½ yd.	Attic Window Blocks
Splash: 1st Border fabric	³⁄₈ yd.	½ yd.	
Splash: 2nd Border fabric	1 yd.	¾ yd.	
Splash: 3rd Border fabric	N/A	1½ yds.	
Binding	½ yd.	⅝ yd.	
Backing	1½ yds.	4 yds.	
Fusible tape	N/A	7½ yds.	

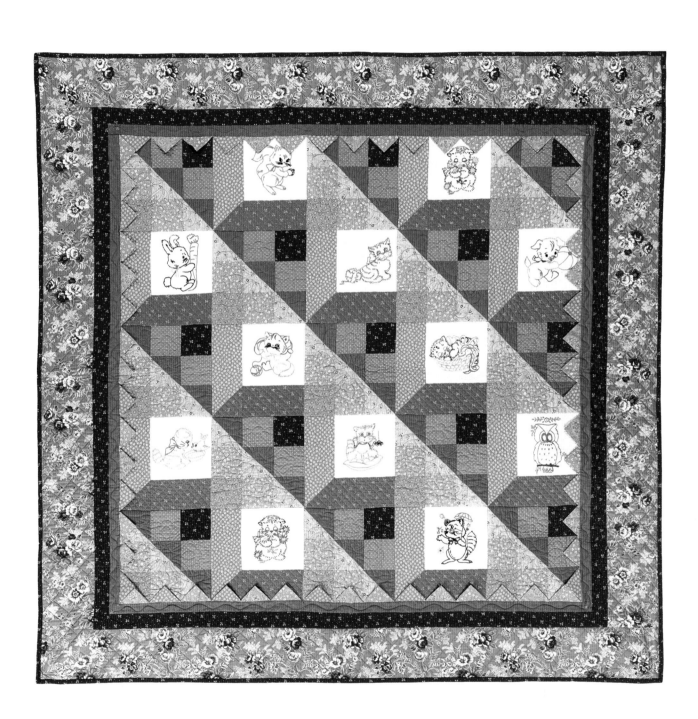

CUTS

FABRIC	CRIB	WALL/LAP
1st Dark fabric (A)	Cut one strip 3½" × 22"; re-cut into six 3½" squares.	Cut two strips 3½" × 42"; re-cut into thirteen 3½" squares.
Medium-dark fabric (B)	Cut one strip 3½" × 42"; re-cut into twelve 3½" squares.	Cut three strips 3½" × 42"; re-cut into twenty-six 3½" squares.
1st Medium fabric (C)	Cut one strip 4" × 42"; re-cut into nine 4" squares.	Cut two strips 4" × 42"; re-cut into twenty 4" squares.
Light fabric (D)	Cut one strip 4" × 42"; re-cut into nine 4" squares.	Cut two strips 4" × 42"; re-cut into twenty 4" squares.
Medium-light fabric (E)	Cut one strip 3½" × 22"; re-cut into six 3½" squares.	Cut two strips 3½" × 42"; re-cut into thirteen 3½" squares.
2nd Light fabric (F)	Cut one strip 3½" × 42"; re-cut into twelve 3½" squares.	Cut three strips 3½" × 42"; re-cut into twenty-six 3½" squares.
2nd Dark fabric (G)	Cut one strip 4" × 13"; re-cut into three 4" squares. Cut one strip 3½" × 42"; re-cut into six rectangles 3½" × 6½".	Cut one strip 4" × 42"; re-cut into six 4" squares. Cut two strips 3½" × 42"; re-cut into twelve rectangles 3½" × 6½".
2nd Medium fabric (H)	Cut one strip 4" × 18"; re-cut into three 4" squares. Cut one strip 3½" × 42½"; re-cut into six rectangles 3½" × 6½"	Cut one strip 14" × 42"; re-cut into six 4" squares. Cut two strips 3½" × 42½"; re-cut into twelve rectangles 3½" × 6½".
Rescued squares or splash fabric (I)	Cut six 6½" squares.	Cut twelve 6½" squares.
1st Border	Cut four strips 1½" × 42" crosswise.	Cut eight strips 2" × 42" crosswise.
2nd Border	Cut four strips 6" × 42" crosswise.	Cut eight strips 2½" × 42" crosswise.
3rd Border fabric	N/A	Cut eight strips 6½" × 42" crosswise.
Folded triangle border	N/A	Cut sixty assorted 3½" squares from the stash fabrics above.
Binding	Cut five strips 2¾" × 42" crosswise.	Cut seven strips 2¾" × 42" crosswise.

MAKE THE HALF-SQUARE UNITS

Use the instructions on pages 16–17 to make the half-square units for the nine-patch blocks and the Attic Window blocks.

1 Make half-squares using your 4" C and D squares for the nine-patch blocks (eighteen half-square units for the crib and thirty-nine half-square units for the wall/lap quilt).

2 Make more half-squares using 4" G and H squares for the Attic Window blocks (six half-square units for the crib and twelve half-square units for the wall/lap quilt) (Figure 1).

Figure 1

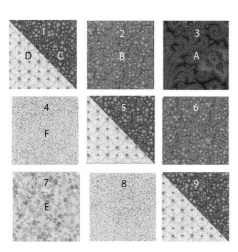

Figure 2

ASSEMBLE THE NINE-PATCH BLOCKS

Note: Change the presser foot to the ¼" foot.

1 Stack all of the nine-patch half-square units and the 3½" A, B, E and F squares for the nine-patch blocks into a nine-patch grid (Figure 2).

2 Use the thread-pinning method (page 14) described in the Techniques section. Following Figure 2, sew 1 to 2, 4 to 5 and 7 to 8 for each block. Then, sew 2 to 3, 5 to 6 and 8 to 9.

3 Sew the three rows together to make each block.

4 Each block should measure 9½", but don't worry if your blocks are smaller. Whatever the common measurement is for the nine-patch block will determine the finished size to trim the Attic Window blocks. Make six nine-patch blocks for the crib quilt and thirteen for the wall/lap quilt.

ASSEMBLE THE ATTIC WINDOW BLOCKS

Note: Use the ¼" presser foot.

1 Stack all the 6½" squares, Attic Window half-squares and 3½" × 6½" rectangles in an unequal four-patch grid (Figure 3).

2 Sew all the 1s to the 2s. Chain-piece them all in order, butting one section against another. Press the seam allowances toward the 1s.

3 Sew all the half-squares for the Attic Window blocks (patch 3) to the rectangles (patch 4). Chain-sew these units together as you did in step 2. Press the seam allowances toward the rectangles. This will set the block up for a staggered seam allowance.

4 Join the 1-2 sections to the 3-4 sections. Chain-piece the final units. Press the seams toward the bottom rectangle. Make six Attic Window blocks for the crib quilt and twelve for the wall/lap quilt.

Figure 3

Figure 4

ASSEMBLE THE QUILT TOP

1 Sew blocks together in horizontal rows. Press seams of joined blocks in one direction. Alternate the direction of seam allowance with each row. Place the seam you want to push toward wrong side up on the ironing board. Set the seam by pressing down on top of the seam. Push the seam in the direction you want it to go from the top side of the quilt to avoid pleats.

2 Join the rows together to complete the quilt top. See Figure 4 for the layout of the crib quilt or Figure 5 for the layout of the wall/lap quilt.

Figure 5

ADD THE BORDERS

Crib Quilt

1 Sew the crosswise strips of the first border to the sides of the quilt. Trim the ends even with the quilt. Press the seams away from the quilt toward the border. Sew the crosswise borders to the top and bottom of the quilt. Cut the ends of the strips even with the edges of the quilt. Press the seams toward the border strips.

2 Add the second border strips to the quilt as outlined in step 1.

Wall/Lap Quilt

1 For all the borders, join the crosswise strips in pairs with a diagonal seam. Use a short stitch (15 stitches per inch). Press the seam allowances open.

2 Refer to page 25 of the Techniques section for instructions on making a folded triangle border from the sixty assorted 3½" squares. There are fifteen triangles on each of the four sides of the quilt. Use a tape measure to space the triangles out on top of the border. Baste the triangles to each border. The triangles are sandwiched in the seam when the borders are sewn to the quilt.

3 Sew the strips of the first border to the sides of the quilt. Trim the ends even with the quilt. Press the seams away from the quilt toward the border. Sew the borders to the top and bottom of the quilt. Cut the ends of the strips even with the edges of the quilt. Press the seams toward the border strips and the triangles toward the quilt.

4 For the two mitered borders, sew pairs of second and third border strips together for a total of four strip pairs.

5 Divide each of the border strips in half and mark the center with a pin. Divide the quilt in half and mark with a pin. Starting at the top of the quilt, match a border pin with the quilt pin. Pin the border in place (Figure 6).

6 Stitch the border onto the quilt from the center out. Use a ¼" seam allowance. Stop sewing ¼" from each corner. Repeat for the bottom border.

7 Press both borders away from the quilt. Flip the quilt over to the wrong side and pin the side borders in place.

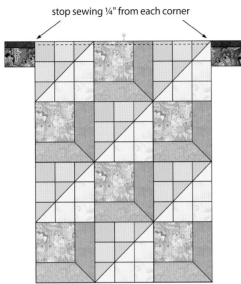

stop sewing ¼" from each corner

Figure 6

11 Tear off a strip of ¼" fusible tape and place it under the top mitered fold at both ends of the top border. Press in place to hold.

12 Fold open the border strip and pin the miter in place. Stitch on the creased line. Open the miter to make sure you have matched each of the borders. Trim the excess border strips with a ½" seam allowance. Press to one side.

13 Repeat this process with the bottom border. See the project photo on page 65 for the final layout of the wall/lap quilt. See Figure 8 for the final layout of the crib quilt.

QUILT AND BIND

8 Stitch the side borders onto the quilt from the center out. Use a ¼" seam allowance. Stop sewing ¼" from each corner. You should be able to see exactly where to stop sewing because the seam side is face up to you (Figure 6).

9 Press both side borders away from the quilt. Stay at the iron to begin the mitering process.

10 Starting with the top border, overlap each end over the top of the side borders. Fold the top border strip back at a 45-degree angle, being careful to align each strip with its matching strip on the corresponding side border. Press in place to create a crease/stitching line (Figure 7).

Figure 8

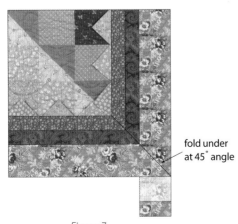

fold under at 45° angle

Figure 7

Whimsy's Butterflies

Pieced by: *Claudia Bissler*

Quilted by: *Janis Hittle*

Quilt Sizes:
Twin: 59" × 77" (shown)
Double: 79" × 97"

Block Size: *9"*

You won't be able to resist my big purple cat and the easy turn appliqué method. Just have fun with this pattern and sew to your heart's content. Get out your stash fabric and choose a value and a color family on the darker side of the color wheel for the hearts/ butterflies. Select any of the complementary hues as the mediums for the half-squares. Choose a bright splash fabric for the light in the half-square blocks. This light will be the dominant color. Make the blocks, sew the quilt together and take it with you to your favorite quilt shop to select just the right splash fabrics for the borders!

YARDAGE

FABRIC	TWIN	DOUBLE	FOR
Splash: Light fabric (A)	2 yds.	3 yds.	Background and 1st Border
Stash: Dark accent fabric (B)	½ yd.	1¼ yds.	Butterflies/Hearts
Stash: Darkest fabric (C)	1 rectangle 9" × 12"	1 fat quarter (optional)	Butterfly Bodies
Stash: Medium accent fabric (D)	½ yd.	1¼ yds.	Butterflies/Hearts
Stash: Medium fabric (E)	1 yd.	2 yds.	Background
Stash: Medium fabric	1 fat quarter or 2" strips from stash (see Make Whimsy the Cat step 1); Scraps of brown and blue for eyes and nose	1 fat quarter or 2" strips from stash (see Make Whimsy the Cat step 1); Scraps of brown and blue for eyes and nose	Whimsy the Cat
Splash: Accent fabric	1 yd.	1¼ yds.	2nd Border
Splash: Dark fabric	2 yds.	2½ yds.	Final Border
Binding	¾ yd.	1 yd.	
Backing	4 yds. of 42" wide or 2 yds. of 90" wide	7¼ yds. of 42" wide or 3 yds. of 90" wide	
Do Sew tracing material	1 yd.	1½ yds.	

CUTS

FABRIC	TWIN	DOUBLE
Light fabric (A)	Cut three strips 10" × 42"; re-cut into twelve 10" squares. Cut six strips 3½" × 42" crosswise.	Cut six strips 10" × 42"; re-cut into twenty-four 10" squares. Cut eight strips 3½" × 42" crosswise.
Dark accent fabric (B)	Cut four strips 3" × 42".	Cut fourteen strips 3" × 42".
Darkest fabric (C)	Cut according to template	Cut according to template
Medium accent fabric (D)	Cut four strips 3" × 42".	Cut fourteen strips 3" × 42".
Medium fabric (E)	Cut three strips 10" × 42"; re-cut into twelve 10" squares.	Cut six strips 10" × 42"; re-cut into twenty-four 10" squares.
Whimsy the Cat fabric	Cut according to templates	Cut according to templates
Border accent fabric	Cut six strips 3" × 42" crosswise.	Cut eight strips 3" × 42" crosswise.
Final border fabric	Cut eight strips 6½" × 42" crosswise.	Cut ten strips 7½" × 42" crosswise.
Binding	Cut seven strips 2¾" × 42".	Cut ten strips 2¾" × 42".

MAKE THE HALF-SQUARE UNITS

1 Use the instructions for making half-square triangles (pages 16–17) to make half-square units from your 10" A and E squares.

2 Press each square open with all seams toward the dark (Figure 1). Make twenty-four blocks for the twin and forty-eight blocks for the double quilt.

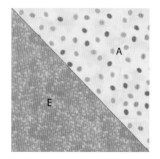

Figure 1

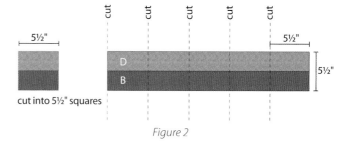

Figure 2

MAKE THE STRIP-SQUARE UNITS

Note: Change the presser foot to the ¼" foot.

1 Sew the 3" × 42" B and D strips together to create strip panels (Figure 2). Make four strip panels for the twin quilt and fourteen for the double quilt. These panels will measure 5½" across when sewn correctly. Press all seams toward the dark.

2 Re-cut panels every 5½" (Figure 2). You need twenty-four strip squares for the twin and ninety-six for the double.

DO SEW HEARTS

1 Trace the heart template onto freezer paper and mark the spots to start and stop stitching. Make several copies. Only the top portion of each heart is stitched to the Do Sew, allowing the bottom raw edge of the heart to get stitched into the seams when blocks are joined.

2 Read the Quick-Turn Appliqué Method on page 21. Cut strips of the Do Sew tracing fabric into 3" × 5½" rectangles. You need twenty-four rectangles for the twin and ninety-six rectangles for the double. Position a Do Sew rectangle at one end of a strip-square, right sides together. Working on the right side of the square, line up the top V and the bottom point of the heart template with the seam of the strip square. The top of the heart should be on top of the Do Sew, and the start and stop spots on the heart template should align with the edge of the Do Sew. The bottom of the heart is not on the Do Sew.

3 Stitch around the top edge of the freezer paper heart, starting from the start spot and ending at the end spot. Be careful not to stitch onto the freezer paper. Remove the paper and use it again. For the twin quilt, stitch twelve hearts with the green/medium on the left side (Figure 3) and twelve hearts with the green/medium on the right side (Figure 4). For the double quilt, stitch forty-eight hearts like Figure 3 and forty-eight hearts like Figure 4.

4 Cut around the heart, leaving a scant ⅛" seam allowance. Notch into the V of the heart. Spritz lightly on top of the Do Sew before turning. Turn the heart right side out from the bottom and press with a steam iron. The Do Sew will roll to the wrong side of the heart. Clip the seam allowance on both sides of the heart where you started and stopped stitching. This allows the seam allowance to lay flat against the raw edge of the block. Repeat for all hearts.

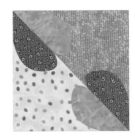
Figure 5

Figure 6

Figure 7

STITCH HEARTS TO HALF-SQUARE UNITS

Position a heart on a half-square unit, with the point of the heart even with the corner of the block. Pin in place. Use a decorative stitch such as a blanket stitch to sew the turned-under top half of the heart to the block. The turned-under edge of the heart is not caught in the seam. Only the bottom raw edges are captured in the seam when blocks are joined. Baste the raw edges of the heart bottom to the block if you wish. For the twin quilt, make four blocks as shown in Figure 5, four blocks as shown in Figure 6, and four blocks as shown in Figure 7. For the double quilt, make forty-eight blocks as shown in Figure 7.

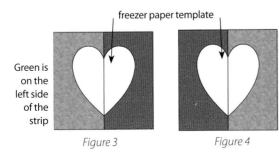

freezer paper template

Green is on the left side of the strip

Figure 3

Green is on the right side of the strip.

Figure 4

Did you know that there're similarities to sewing and driving on mountain roads? When driving on the switchback roads, you go slow and downshift. When sewing inside curves and sharp angles, sew slow and set your machine at a shorter stitch length. (I compare the shorter stitch length to downshifting!) These two adjustments will make it easier to achieve a smoothly shaped Whimsy the Cat appliqué.

NOTES FROM **NANCY**

Figure 8

Figure 9

ASSEMBLE THE QUILT TOP

1 For the double quilt, sew the blocks together in groups of four (Figure 9), turning them as shown. Join the large blocks in four rows (Figure 11).

2 For the twin quilt, sew the blocks together in six horizontal rows, turning blocks as necessary and positioning the hearts as shown (Figure 10). Press the seam allowances in opposing directions in alternating rows. Join the rows.

3 For the twin quilt, stitch Whimsy to the center of the quilt (Figure 10). Add the facial details. Use a blind hemstitch or other decorative stitch to accent Whimsy. If you desire, stitch Whimsy to the bottom right corner of the double quilt after the borders are added.3the seam. Push the seam in the direction you want it to go from the top side of the quilt to avoid pleats.

MAKE WHIMSY THE CAT

1 Whimsy is your fantasy cat. Make him or her any color you desire. I stitched a panel made of ten strips 2" wide by 22" long. All the strips were sewn together on their long sides and seams were all pressed in one direction. Then I placed the Whimsy template on top and cut around it. The end result produced a more dimensional cat. You could use strips of several different fabrics from your stash to make the cat or substitute a fat quarter of the same fabric if you don't want to piece him. The strips just add a little dimensionality.

2 Enlarge the templates as instructed on pages 76-77. Trace templates onto freezer paper. Cut a piece of Do Sew the same size as the fat quarter or the strip pieced panel.

3 Put the Do Sew right sides together with the strip pieced panel or fabric. Iron the templates to the right side of the fabric. Stitch around the outside edges of the freezer paper templates. Trim the seam allowance to ⅛" or less. Notch into the deep curve of the tail of the cat. Spritz lightly on top of the Do Sew before turning. Cut a small hole into the Do Sew on each patch. Turn right side out and press with steam iron. The Do Sew should roll under to the wrong side of the fabric.

Figure 10

Figure 11

ADD THE BORDERS

1 For all borders, join the strips in pairs with a diagonal seam. Use a short stitch (15 stitches per inch). Press the seams open. Add a third strip to two of the pairs for the sides of the double quilt.

2 Sew the shorter borders to the top and bottom of the quilt. Press the seams toward the border strips. Cut the ends of the strips even with the edges of the quilt.

3 Sew the remaining borders to the sides of the quilt. Press the seams toward the border strips. Cut the ends of the strips even with the edges of the quilt.

ADD THE BUTTERFLY BODIES

You can choose to add the butterfly bodies or eliminate them.

1 Remove one of the release papers from the Do Sew to expose the tacky surface. Save this paper! Smooth the tacky surface of the fusible web by hand onto the wrong side of the 9" × 12" rectangle of fabric you've chosen for the butterfly bodies.

2 Steam-press the fusible web to the back side of the rectangle. Do not remove the final release paper from the back side just yet.

3 Trace the butterfly body onto freezer paper. Cut out the body, leaving extra paper around it. Press the butterfly template to the right side of the prepared fabric. Cut the butterfly body on the drawn lines. Cut sixteen bodies.

4 Remove the freezer paper template. Pull the paper backing off the butterfly body and position the body between two heart wings, referring to the finished quilt on page 71. Press with a steam iron to secure to the quilt. Repeat with all bodies.

5 To give the bodies dimension, refer to 3-D Appliqué Method on pages 22-23. Place a small scrap of thin cotton batting on the backside of the quilt under each body. Stitch the body in place with a decorative stitch. To create the antennae, first draw with a marker, and then sew with a straight-stitch or narrow zigzag over the marking. Trim the excess batting from around the body on the back of the quilt. Repeat on all butterflies.

QUILT AND BIND

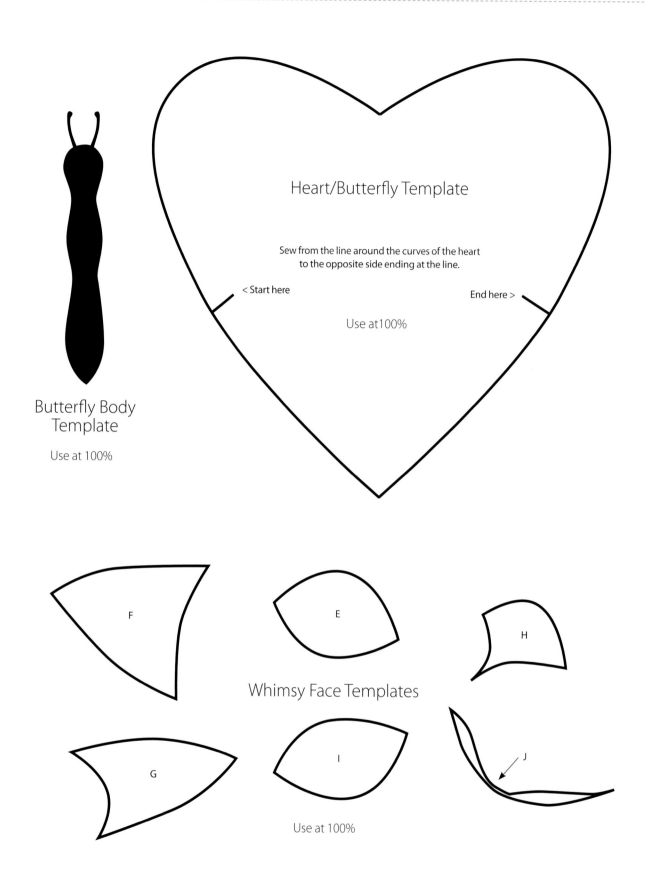

Butterfly Body
Template

Use at 100%

Heart/Butterfly Template

Sew from the line around the curves of the heart
to the opposite side ending at the line.

< Start here

End here >

Use at 100%

Whimsy Face Templates

F

E

H

G

I

J

Use at 100%

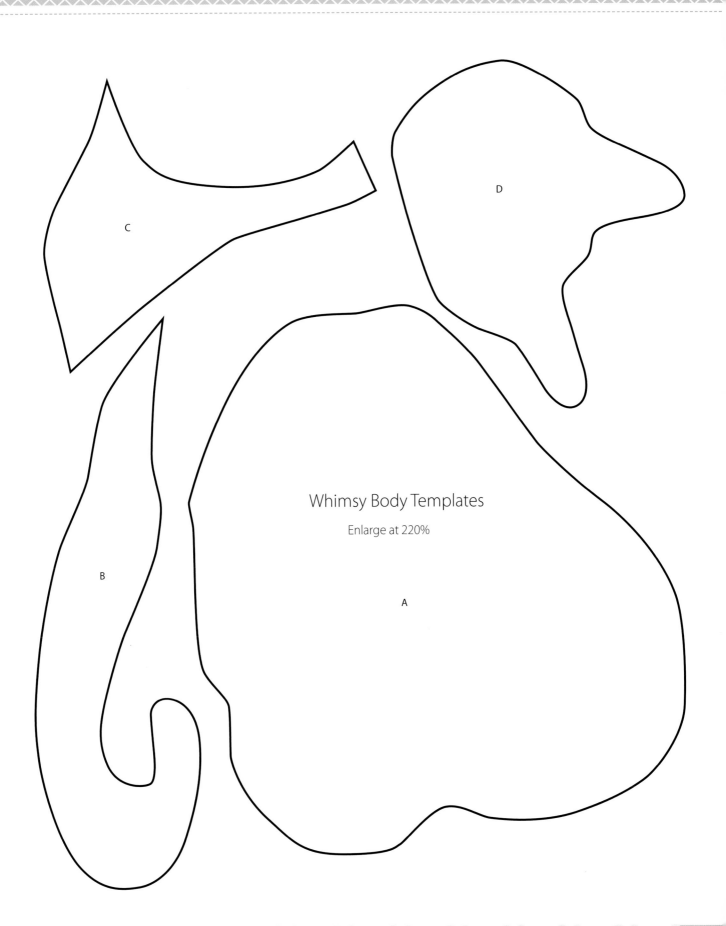

Whimsy Body Templates

Enlarge at 220%

❧ 4 ❧

quilts from fat quarters

I don't know about you but at every quilt shop I visit and every quilt show I attend, the first thing I buy is fat quarters. So I have plenty of these little beauties in my stash. It just made sense to me to develop some patterns that call for fat quarters.

The first quilts in the chapter are the *Four-Patch Twins*. These two quilts were so much fun to make. I love the way the blocks twist and turn to develop the pattern. Try twisting and turning your blocks and you may discover even more layouts for these quilt designs.

Have you ever gone on a cruise or spent some time in the sunny state of Florida? *Caribbean Splash* might just be the quilt to remind you of your sun-drenched holiday. This quilt combines two blocks: the Greek Cross and Card Trick.

Ribbons of Valor is a tribute quilt that you can make for anyone you know who has served time in the armed forces. While I'm writing this book, our country is at war in Afghanistan and so many of our young men and women are giving their time and lives to keep us safe at home. This quilt might be a great way to honor someone you know. There are several quilt guilds and organizations across the country making quilts for wounded soldiers returning home from overseas. One such group that is making a difference is called "Quilts of Valor."

Four-Patch Twins I & II

Pieced by: *Claudia Bissler*

Quilted by: *Nancy Gano*

Quilt Sizes:
Twin I: 51" × 63"
(shown, below left)
Twin II: 53½" × 70½"
(shown, below right)

Block Size: *12"*

I started this project by making a couple of blocks and quickly realized that just a simple flip and flop of certain pieces created an additional block that was a mirror image of the first block. These two quilts would really be fun to make with your best quilting buddy. Imagine sharing your stash and then finding just the right splash fabrics together. You could start out with the same fabrics and each of you would have a similar, but not identical, quilt.

Any color scheme you choose will work with these quilts; just exchange the black and white fat quarters for any light and dark fat quarters that you have on hand. The splash in these quilts is the green and red accent fabrics along with the final border. I found the floral border fabric first and then decided on the accent pieces.

YARDAGE

FABRIC	TWIN I	TWIN II	FOR
Stash: White fabrics (A)	4 fat quarters	4 fat quarters	Criss-Cross Blocks and Pieced Border
Stash: Black fabrics (B)	4 fat quarters	4 fat quarters	Criss-Cross Blocks and Pieced Border
Splash: Green fabric (C)	1 yd.	1 yd.	Accents and Border
Splash: Red fabric (D)	1 yd.	1 yd.	Accents and Border
Splash: 3rd Accent fabric (E)	2 yds.	2 yds.	Outer Border
Stash: Black print fabric (F)	N/A	⅞ yd.	Setting Triangles
Binding	⅝ yd.	⅝ yd.	Binding
Backing	4 yds. of 42" wide	4½ yds. of 42" wide	

CUTS

FABRIC	FOUR-PATCH TWIN I	FOUR-PATCH TWIN II
Fabric A	From each, cut one strip 7½" × 21" (four total). From each, cut two strips 5" × 21"; re-cut each strip into four or five rectangles 2¾" × 5" (thirty-four total). From each, cut one 2¾" square (four total).	From each, cut one strip 7½" × 21" (four total). From each, cut two strips 5½" × 21"; re-cut each strip into four or five rectangles 2¾" × 5" (thirty-six total). From each, cut one 2¾" square (four total).
Fabric B	From each, cut one strip 10¼" × 21"; re-cut strip into two 10¼" squares; re-cut squares into thirty-two quarter-square triangles. (See Begin the Blocks steps 3–4 on page 82.) From each, cut one strip 6½" × 21"; re-cut into five rectangles 2¾" × 6½" (twenty total). From each, cut one 2¾" square (four total).	From each, cut one strip 10¼" × 21"; re-cut strip into two 10¼" squares; re-cut squares into thirty-two quarter-square triangles. (See Begin the Blocks steps 3–4 on page 82.)
Fabric C	Cut one strip 2¾" × 42", then cut strip in half. Cut eight strips 2" × 42" crosswise.	Cut one strip 2¾" × 42", then cut strip in half. Cut four strips 2" × 32". Cut four strips 2" × 18".
Fabric D	Cut one strip 2¾" × 42", then cut strip in half. Cut eight strips 2" × 42" crosswise.	Cut one strip 2¾" × 42", then cut strip in half. Cut four strips 2" × 42" crosswise.
Fabric E	Cut six strips 6½" × 42" crosswise.	Cut six strips 6½" × 42" crosswise.
Fabric F	N/A	Cut one strip 19" × 42"; re-cut into two 19" squares. Cut one strip 9½" × 42"; re-cut into two triangles following instructions in Techniques (page 12) for cutting setting triangles from strips; triangles will be 9½" high with a 19" base.
Binding	Cut six strips 2¾" × 42".	Cut seven strips 2¾" × 42".

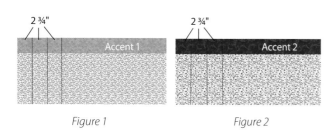

Figure 1　　　　　　　　　　　Figure 2

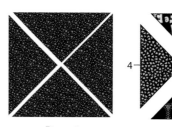 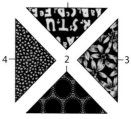

Figure 3　　　　　　　　　　Figure 4

BEGIN THE CRISS-CROSS BLOCKS

1 Stitch the 2¾" C and D strips to the 7½" A strips. Make two of these bands with fabric C and press seams toward the A strips (Figure 1). Make two bands with fabric D and press seams toward the D strip (Figure 2).

2 Re-cut each of the bands into 2¾" segments. Cut six segments from each band (twenty-four total) for Twin I or cut seven segments from each (twenty-eight total) for Twin II. Divide the segments into eight stacks with either three or four of the same color segments in each. Half of the stacks are for Block A and half are for Block B.

3 Cut two 10¼" squares from each of the black fat quarters. Stack the squares in two piles, each pile with one of the four fabrics stacked in the same order.

4 Keep all of the squares in the pile with the lengthwise grains on the left and right side. This will place the crosswise grains on the top and bottom of the pile. Re-cut the 10¼" squares twice on the diagonal (Figure 3).

5 Working clockwise from the top pile, remove the first triangle and place it on the bottom of the pile.

6 From the right-side pile, remove the top two triangles and place them on the bottom of the pile.

7 From the bottom pile, remove the top three triangles and place them on the bottom of the pile.

8 Leave the left-side pile alone. All the triangles on the top of the piles should be different fabrics (Figure 4).

9 Repeat this process for both piles of triangles. Keep the stacks for the different blocks separate.

MAKE THE A BLOCKS

1 You have two stacks of triangles with four triangles in each individual pile. Use stick-on labels and mark the triangles in each pile with the following identities; 1 (top), 2 (bottom), 3 (right-side), 4 (left-side).

2 This step is extremely important so take your time and lay out the blocks exactly as shown (Figure 5). The triangles should point to the left.

Four-Patch Twin I

a. Place one stack of three green strip segments with triangle pile 1.

b. Place one stack of three green strip segments with triangle pile 3.

c. Place one stack of three red strip segments with triangle pile 2.

d. Place one stack of three red strip segments with triangle pile 4.

Four-Patch Twin II

a. Place one stack of four green strip segments with triangle pile 1.

b. Place one stack of four green strip segments with triangle pile 3.

c. Place one stack of four red strip segments with triangle pile 2.

d. Place one stack of four red strip segments with triangle pile 4.

Pile 1　　　　Pile 3　　　　Pile 2　　　　Pile 4

Figure 5 (for A Blocks)

3 Stitch each of the strip segments to the triangles by flipping the strip segments right sides together with the triangles. Keep the triangles pointed to the left in the pile. Chain-sew these units one strip segment and triangle pile at a time keeping the threads between the units. This will keep the piles together and make it easier to assemble the A blocks. Press the seam allowance toward the dark triangles. Return each group of sewn triangles and strip segments back to the original block rotation.

4 Stitch pile 1 units and pile 2 units together and pile 3 units and pile 4 units together to form larger triangles (Figure 6). Press the seams to the dark triangle.

5 Stitch the combined piles of 1 and 2 with the piles of 3 and 4 together to make Block A. You will have enough to make four A blocks (Figure 7). Make three A blocks for Twin I and four A blocks for Twin II.

6 Fold blocks in half on the diagonal to trim off the extensions of the rectangles (Figure 8).

MAKE THE B BLOCKS

1 The remaining group of black quarter-square triangles should be marked as shown in Figure 4.

2 This step is extremely important, so take your time and lay out the blocks exactly as shown (Figure 9). The triangles should point to the right.

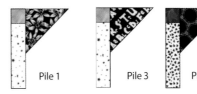

Pile 1   Pile 3   Pile 2   Pile 4

Figure 9 (for B Blocks)

Four-Patch Twin I

a. Place one stack of three green strip segments with triangle pile 1.

b. Place one stack of three green strip segments with triangle pile 3.

c. Place one stack of three red strip segments with triangle pile 2.

d. Place one stack of three red strip segments with triangle pile 4.

Four-Patch Twin II

a. Place one stack of four green strip segments with triangle pile 1.

b. Place one stack of four green strip segments with triangle pile 3.

c. Place one stack of four red strip segments with triangle pile 2.

d. Place one stack of four red strip segments with triangle pile 4.

3 Stitch each of the strip segments to the triangles as you did for the A blocks, but keep the triangles pointing to the right. Press the seam allowance toward the dark triangles.

4 Sew the triangles into larger triangles, sew triangles into blocks, and trim as described in Make the A Block steps 4-6. See Figures 10 and 11. You will need three B Blocks for either the Twin I or Twin II quilt.

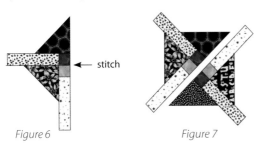

← stitch

Figure 6   *Figure 7*

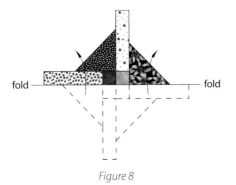

fold — — — fold

Figure 8

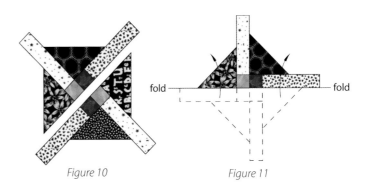

fold — — — fold

Figure 10   *Figure 11*

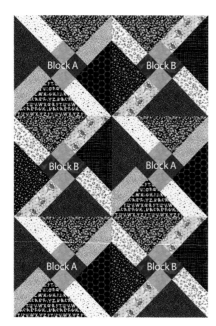

Figure 12

ASSEMBLE THE QUILT TOP

Four-Patch Twin I

1. Sew the blocks together in horizontal rows. Join the rows together to complete the quilt top (Figure 12). Notice that you will use three each of Block A and Block B, alternating their position in the row to form the links in the pattern.

2. Press the seams of the joined blocks in one direction. Alternate the direction of the seam allowance with each row. Join the rows.

Four-Patch Twin II

1. The first border in this quilt is added to the black setting triangles on the corners and sides of the quilt. Sew a 2" × 18" C border strip to both short sides of the two side triangles (Figure 13). Set aside.

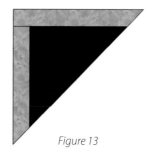

Figure 13

2. Cut the two black 19" squares in half diagonally. Sew a 2" C strip to the long edge of each large corner triangle. Measure up from the bottom edge of the triangle 1½". Draw a vertical line. Place the long side of the strip on the line (Figure 14). Sew ¼" from the line. Press the strip down toward the bottom of the triangle. Trim the edges of the strip to match the triangles. (Figure 15).

3. Arrange four A Blocks, three B Blocks, and two side triangles in diagonal rows (Figure 16). Be sure to check the orientation of the red and green squares in the block centers. Sew the parts into three rows, matching seams carefully. Join the rows.

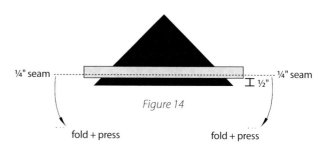

¼" seam — — — ¼" seam

⊥ ½"

fold + press   fold + press

Figure 14

Mark 1½" up from the bottom of the triangle.

1½"

Figure 15

Figure 16

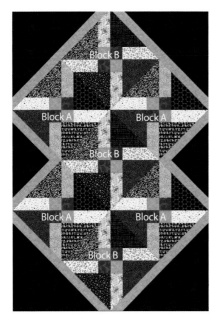

Figure 17

4 Mark the center of the long edge of the green strip on each corner triangle. With right sides together, place a corner triangle on top of the corner of the quilt, matching the center mark with the seam between the A and B blocks. Sew the pieced corner triangle to the quilt. Repeat on all four corners. Press the corner triangles away from the quilt.

5 Trim the edges of the quilt, making sure the corners are ninety-degrees (Figure 17).

ADD THE BORDERS

Four-Patch Twin I

1 For the first pieced border, stitch together six 2¾" × 6½" B rectangles. Sew to the side of the quilt. Repeat for the other side. Press the seam allowances toward the quilt.

2 Stitch four 2¾" × 6½" B rectangles together. Sew a 2¾" B square to each end. Repeat to make a second border. Sew to the top and bottom of the quilt.

3 For the second splash fabric border, join the crosswise C strips in pairs with a diagonal seam. Use a short stitch (15 stitches per inch). Press the seams open. Make four borders like this. Sew borders to the sides of the quilt. Trim the ends of the strips even with the edges of the quilt. Press the seams toward the border strip. Sew borders to the top and bottom of the quilt. Trim even with the quilt.

4 For the third pieced border, stitch ten 2¾" × 5" A rectangles together. Matching the center of the border with the center of the quilt, sew the border to the side of the quilt. Trim the border even with the quilt's edges. Repeat for the other side. Press the borders away from the quilt.

5 Join seven 2¾" × 5" A rectangles together. Add a 2¾" A square to each end. Make two borders. Sew to the top and bottom of the quilt.

6 For the fourth and fifth splash fabric borders, repeat step 3. See the project photo on page 80 for the final layout of the quilt.

Figure 18

Four-Patch Twin II

1 For the first pieced border, stitch seven 2¾" × 5½" A rectangles together. Sew a 2¾" A square to each end (Figure 18). Repeat to make another border. Set aside.

2 Stitch eleven A rectangles together. Make two borders. Matching centers of the long borders with the center of the quilt, sew the long borders to the sides of the quilt. Trim the ends even with the quilt. Press the seam allowances toward the quilt. Sew the shorter borders to the top and bottom of the quilt.

3 For the second border, join 1½" D strips with a diagonal seam. Use a short stitch (15 stitches per inch). Press the seams open. Make four borders like this. Sew borders to the sides of the quilt. Press border away from the quilt. Trim the ends even with the quilt. Sew borders to the top and bottom of the quilt. Trim even with the quilt.

4 For the third border, join 1½" E strips for each border. Sew to the sides and trim even with the quilt. Add the top and bottom borders and trim.

QUILT AND BIND

Caribbean Splash

Pieced by: *Claudia Bissler*

Quilted by: *Janis Hittle*

Quilt Sizes:
Lap: 54" × 66" (shown)
Queen: 83" × 107"

Block Size: *12"*

This quilt is all about combining bright happy colors from your stash in two blocks that alternate across and down the quilt. Start sorting through your stash and select your brightest, boldest stash fabrics to audition for this production. Here's a chance to use up those wonderful fat quarters you've been collecting in your stash. I chose to use a lot of bright fabrics, but any fabric collection will work. I took my fat quarters to my local quilt shop and selected some splash fabrics for the borders. The main border is incorporated into the Greek Cross block in the center square.

YARDAGE

FABRIC	LAP	QUEEN	FOR
Stash: Yellow/blue fabric (A)	2 fat quarters or ½ yd.	3 fat quarters or ¾ yd.	Card Trick Blocks
Stash: Pink fabric (B)	2 fat quarters or ½ yd.	3 fat quarters or ¾ yd.	Card Trick Blocks
Stash: Green fabric (C)	2 fat quarters or ½ yd.	3 fat quarters or ¾ yd.	Card Trick Blocks
Stash: Purple fabric (D)	2 fat quarters or ½ yd.	3 fat quarters or ¾ yd.	Card Trick Blocks
Stash: Turquoise fabric (E)	2 fat quarters or ½ yd.	1½ yds.	Greek Cross and Card Trick Blocks
Stash: Pale yellow fabric (F)	3 fat quarters or ¾ yd.	2¼ yds.	Greek Cross and Card Trick Blocks
Stash: Contrast fabric (G)	1 fat quarter or ¼ yd.	3 fat quarters or ¾ yd.	Greek Cross Blocks
Splash: Splash fabric (H)	1 fat quarter or ¼ yd.	2 fat quarters or ½ yd.	Greek Cross Blocks
Splash: 1st Border fabric	³/₈ yd	¾ yd.	
Splash: 2nd Border fabric	¾ yd.	1 yd.	
Splash: 3rd Border fabric	1 ½ yd.	2¾ yds.	
Binding	⁵/₈ yd.	1 yd.	
Backing	4 yds. of 42" wide fabric	7¾ yds. of 42" wide or 3½ yds. of 90" wide	

CUTS

FABRIC	LAP	QUEEN
Fabric A	Cut two strips 5" × 21"; re-cut into seven 5" squares. Cut two strips 5½" × 21"; re-cut into four 5½" squares.	Cut five strips 5" × 21"; re-cut into nineteen 5" squares. Cut four strips 5½" × 21"; re-cut into ten 5½" squares.
Fabric B	Cut two strips 5" × 21"; re-cut into seven 5" squares. Cut two strips 5½" × 21"; re-cut into four 5½" squares.	Cut five strips 5" × 21"; re-cut into nineteen 5" squares. Cut four strips 5½" × 21"; re-cut into ten 5½" squares.
Fabric C	Cut two strips 5" × 21"; re-cut into seven 5" squares. Cut two strips 5½" × 21"; re-cut into four 5½" squares.	Cut five strips 5" × 21"; re-cut into nineteen 5" squares. Cut four strips 5½" × 21"; re-cut into ten 5½" squares.
Fabric D	Cut two strips 5" × 21"; re-cut into seven 5" squares. Cut two strips 5½" × 21"; re-cut into four 5½" squares.	Cut five strips 5" × 21"; re-cut into nineteen 5" squares. Cut four strips 5½" × 21"; re-cut into ten 5½" squares.
Fabric E	Cut three strips 5" × 21"; re-cut into twelve 5" squares. Cut three strips 5½" × 21"; re-cut into eight 5½" squares.	Cut five strips 5" × 42"; re-cut into thirty-six 5" squares. Cut 3 strips 5½" × 42"; re-cut into twenty 5½" squares.
Fabric F	Cut six strips 5" × 21"; re-cut into twenty-four 5" squares. Cut six strips 2½" × 21".	Cut nine strips 5" × 42"; re-cut into seventy-two 5" squares. Cut eighteen strips 2½" × 21" or nine strips 2½" × 42".
Fabric G	Cut six strips 2½" × 21".	Cut eighteen strips 2½" × 21" or nine strips 2½" × 42".
Fabric H	Cut two strips 4½" × 21"; re-cut into six 4½" squares.	Cut five strips 4½" × 21" or three strips 4½" × 42"; re-cut into eighteen 4½" squares.
1st Border	Cut six strips 1½" × 42" crosswise.	Cut eight strips 2" × 42" crosswise.
2nd Border	Cut six strips 2½" × 42" crosswise.	Cut ten strips 3" × 42" crosswise.
3rd Border	Cut three strips 6½" × 42" crosswise; cut one strip in half and sew each half onto the other strips. Cut four strips 6½" × 34" lengthwise from remaining fabric.	Cut five strips 8" × 42" crosswise; cut one strip in half and sew each half onto the pairs. Cut four strips 8" × 55" lengthwise from remaining fabric.
Binding	Cut six strips 2¾" × 42".	Cut ten strips 2¾" × 42".

MAKE THE HALF-SQUARE UNITS

Make these units using a ⅜" seam allowance. Adjust your needle position if necessary.

1. Refer to pages 16-17 to make half-square units. Join twelve 5" F squares with three each of the 5" A, B, C, and D squares. Make six half-square units with each of the four colors (twenty-four total) for the lap quilt Card Trick blocks (Figure 1). For the queen quilt, use thirty-six F squares and nine each of the A, B, C, and D squares to make seventeen units in each color combination (sixty-eight total). Note that there will be one leftover unit of each color when you make the units for the queen quilt. Set units aside.

2. Sew twelve 5" E squares with twelve 5" F squares to make twenty-four half-square units for the lap quilt Greek Cross blocks (Figure 2). Make seventy-two half-square units with thirty-six E and thirty-six F squares for the queen quilt Greek Cross blocks. Set aside.

MAKE THE QUARTER-SQUARE UNITS

1. Quarter-square units are made with these combinations using 5½" squares: A square with B square; C square with D square. Refer to pages 16-17 to make four half-square units of each color combination (eight total) for the lap quilt. Make ten half-square units of each color combination (twenty total) for the queen quilt. Press the seam allowances toward the B and D triangles.

2. Refer to pages 17-18 to turn the half-square units into the quarter-square units needed for the centers of the Card Trick blocks. Lay an A-B half-square unit on top of a C-D unit, with the B patch on top of the C patch. Draw a diagonal line across the seam on the wrong side of a unit, and stitch ⅜" away from each side of the drawn line. Cut on the drawn line to make two quarter-square units that are mirror images of each other (Figure 3). Keep three of each kind for the lap quilt and nine of each kind for the queen quilt. Some units are not needed.

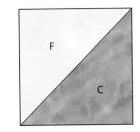
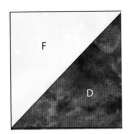

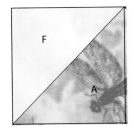

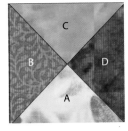

Figure 1

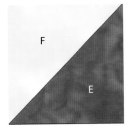

Figure 2

Figure 3

MAKE THE 3-PART SQUARE UNITS

1 These units are a combination of one half-square unit and one whole square, so you end up with a three-part unit. Refer to pages 16-17 to make half-square units with these four combinations using 5½" squares: Sew eight turqoise E squares with two squares each of the A, B, C and D fabrics for the lap quilt. You will get four A/E, four B/E, four C/E and four D/E half-square units. Sew twenty E squares with five squares each of the A, B, C and D fabrics for the queen quilt. You will get ten half-square units in each color combination.

2 Make stacks of each color of half-square units and plain squares to keep from mixing up the colors. Draw a diagonal line on the back of each plain square. Referring to Figure 4 for color combinations, position the plain square on top of the half-square unit right sides together so that the drawn line crosses the seam of the half-square unit underneath. Stitch along both sides of the drawn line. Cut apart on the drawn line to get two 3-part units that are mirror images of each other (Figure 4). Repeat with each color combination.

3 For the lap quilt, make twenty-four total 3-part squares for the lap quilt, six of each combination. Make sixty-eight total three-part squares for the queen quilt, seventeen of each combination. Some units will not be needed.

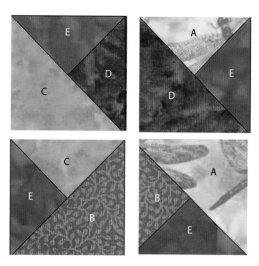

Figure 4

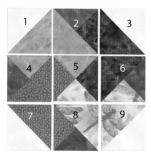

Figure 5

ASSEMBLE THE CARD TRICK BLOCKS

Note: The seam allowances for the blocks are ¼".

1 Refer to Figure 5 to arrange the appropriate half-square units, three-part units, and the center quarter-square units in a nine-patch grid, or try alternating the arrangement of these blocks, as shown in the quilt on page 87. Join the squares for each row following Making a Nine-Patch Block on page 19. Press the seam in each row towards the three-part squares.

2 Sew the three rows together to make a block. Press the two final seams away from the center row. Make six for the lap quilt. Make seventeen blocks for the queen quilt. Note that there will be some units leftover from each quilt.

3 Each block should measure 12½". However, the common measurement for the Card Trick block determines the finished size to trim the Greek Cross blocks.

MAKE THE GREEK CROSS BLOCKS

Note: The seam allowances for the blocks are ¼".

1 Sew 2½" × 21" F and G strips together to create the strip bands (Figure 7). Make six bands for the lap quilt and eighteen bands for the queen quilt. Press seams toward the dark strips. The bands should measure 4½" across. Re-cut bands every 4½". You need twenty-four strip squares for the lap quilt and seventy-two strip squares for the queen.

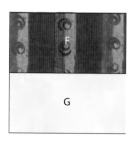

Figure 7

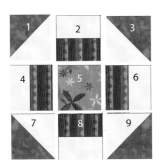

Figure 8		*Figure 9*

2 For this block you need the strip squares, plus the twenty-four E/F half-square units (shown in Figure 2) for the lap quilt and 72 E/F half-squares for the queen quilt. You need six 4½" H squares for the lap and eighteen H squares for the queen quilt. Join the squares in three horizontal rows following Figure 8. Make six blocks for the lap quilt and eighteen blocks for the queen (Figure 9).

3 After pressing, measure the Greek Cross blocks. Trim the blocks the same size as the Card Trick blocks, if necessary.

ASSEMBLE THE QUILT TOP AND ADD THE BORDERS

1 Sew the blocks together in horizontal rows, referring to Figure 10 for the lap quilt and Figure 11 for the queen quilt. Press the seams in alternating rows in opposite directions. Refer to the pressing instructions on page 14. Join the rows.

2 For each border, join crosswise strips together with a diagonal seam. Cut some strips in half, and sew each half onto the other strips where needed to make the borders long enough. Use a short stitch (15 stitches per inch). For the outer border, join the lengthwise strips in pairs. Press the seams open.

3 Sew the first longer border strips to the sides of the quilt. Trim the ends even with the quilt. Press the seams away from the quilt toward the border. Sew the shorter borders to the top and bottom. Trim. Repeat for the remaining borders.

QUILT AND BIND

Figure 10

Figure 11

Ribbons of Valor

Pieced by: *Claudia Bissler*

Quilted by: *Nancy Gano*

Quilt Sizes:
Crib: 36½" × 49¼"
Twin: 60¼" × 73" (shown)

Block Size: *9"*

My husband is a veteran like so many of the men and women in your life and I wanted to make a quilt that could be used for a returning veteran or anyone you know who would appreciate it. I combined stars and ribbons to create a patriotic feeling in this quilt.

This simple block has a lot of movement when you mix dark, medium and light backgrounds. The star blocks are made entirely of stash fabrics. Once the blocks were made it was time to go shopping. What fun! Strangely enough, I experienced no guilt as I purchased my splash fabrics for the setting triangles and borders.

YARDAGE

FABRIC	CRIB	LAP	FOR
Stash: Light tan fabric (A)	N/A	1 fat quarter	Block B
Stash: Dark navy print (B)	1 fat quarter	3 fat quarters	Blocks A and B
Stash: Navy print (C)	1 fat quarter	2 fat quarters	Blocks A and B
Stash: Red print (D)	1 fat quarter	2 fat quarters	Block A
Stash: Gold print (E)	1 fat quarter	3 fat quarters	Blocks A and B
Stash: Light gold print (F)	1 fat quarter	1 fat quarter	Blocks A and B
Splash: Setting triangle fabric (G)	⅝ yd.	1 yd.	Setting Triangles
Splash: Dark accent fabric (H)	¼ yd.	1 yd.	Inner Border
Splash: Medium accent fabric (I)	1 yd.	2 yds.	Outer Border
Binding	½ yd.	¾ yd.	
Backing	1¾ yds. of 42" wide fabric	4½ yds. of 42" wide fabric	

CUTS

FABRIC	CRIB	LAP
Fabric A	N/A	Cut twelve 4" squares. Cut three strips 2½" × 21".
Fabric B	Cut sixteen 4" squares.	Cut thirty-six 4" squares. Cut five strips 2½" × 21"; re-cut into fourteen rectangles 2½" × 6½". Cut four 2½" squares.
Fabric C	Cut sixteen 4" squares.	Cut thirty-six 4" squares.
Fabric D	Cut sixteen 4" squares.	Cut twenty-four 4" squares. Cut three strips 2½" × 21".
Fabric E	Cut sixteen 4" squares.	Cut thirty-six 4" squares. Cut three strips 2½" × 21".
Fabric F	Cut eight squares 3½".	Cut eighteen 3½" squares.
Fabric G	Cut two strips 7½" × 42". Cut two squares 8½"; re-cut into four half-square triangles.	Cut three strips 7½" × 42". Cut two squares 8½"; re-cut into four half-square triangles.
Fabric H	Cut four strips 2" × 42" crosswise.	Cut twelve strips 2" × 42" crosswise.
Fabric I	Cut two strips 4½" × 42" crosswise. Cut four strips 4½" × 42" lengthwise from remaining fabric.	Cut four strips 6½" × 42" crosswise. Cut four strips 6½" × 42" lengthwise from remaining fabric.
Binding	Cut six strips 2¾" × 42".	Cut seven strips 2¾" × 42".

MAKE THE HALF-SQUARE UNITS

1 Follow the instructions on pages 16–17 for making half-square triangle units. Use a ⅜" seam allowance when making these units. Pair the C and D squares and the B and E squares. For the crib quilt, make thirty-two B/E units (Figure 1) and thirty-two C/D units (Figure 2). For the lap quilt, make forty-eight B/E units and forty-eight C/D units.

2 For the lap quilt, repeat step 1 to create twenty-four additional B/E units and twenty-four A/C units (Figure 3) for the B blocks.

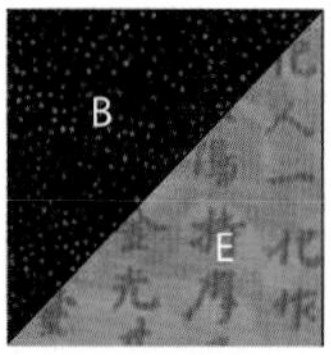

Figure 1

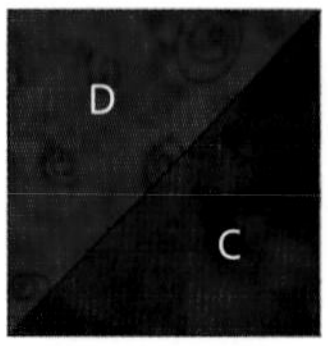

Figure 2

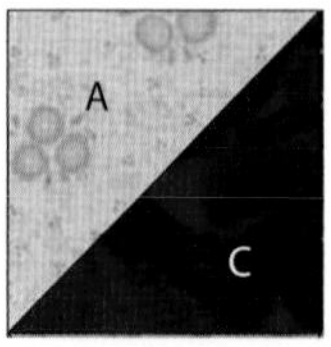

Figure 3

MAKE THE FRIENDSHIP STAR BLOCKS

Note: Change the presser foot to the ¼" foot.

1 Follow instructions for making nine-patch blocks (page 19). Stack all the squares into a nine-patch grid. Follow Figure 4 for A blocks and Figure 5 for B blocks.

2 Stitch the squares together following their numbered order in the grid to form horizontal rows. Use the thread-pinning method. Make three horizontal rows. Press the seams in the top and bottom row away from the middle unit. Press the center row toward the center square.

3 Sew the three rows together to make the block. The seams should all be in opposing directions. Press the two final seams towards the center row. Each block should measure 9½". Make eight A blocks for the crib quilt. Make twelve A blocks and six B blocks for the lap quilt.

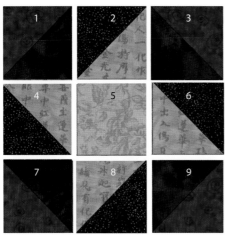

Figure 4

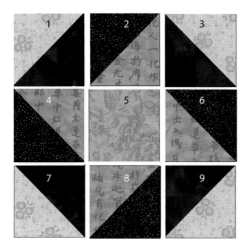

Figure 5

Figure 6

Figure 7

ASSEMBLE THE QUILT TOP

1 Follow instructions for cutting setting triangles in the Techniques section (page 12). From each of the 7½" × 42" G strips, cut three or four setting triangles. You need six setting triangles for the crib quilt and ten setting triangles for the lap quilt. Cut the 8½" G squares diagonally once to make the corner triangles.

2 Sew blocks together in diagonal rows. Follow the numbered piecing order in the layout diagram (Figure 6 for the lap quilt and Figure 7 for the crib quilt). You need a total of eight of Block A and six setting triangles plus four corner triangles for the crib quilt (Figure 6). You need a total of twelve Block A and six Block B plus ten setting triangles and four corner triangles for the lap quilt (Figure 7).

NOTES FROM **NANCY**

Cindy demonstrates the quilt process on the *Stash With Splash Quilts* DVD. It's exciting to see how fat quarter cuts of fabric can turn into a stunning quilt. When you insert the DVD into your TV or computer, click on Quilts from Fat Quarters for a personalized lesson.

Figure 8

3 Join the rows together with setting triangles to complete the quilt top.

4 Press the seams of joined blocks in one direction. Alternate the direction of the seam allowance with each row. Place the seam you want to push toward the wrong side up on the ironing board. Set the seam by pressing down on top of the seam. Push the seam in the direction you want it to go from the top side of the quilt to avoid pleats.

ADD BORDERS

Crib Quilt

1 For the first border, sew the H border strips to the sides of the quilt. Trim the ends even with the quilt. Press the seams away from the quilt. Sew the H borders to the top and bottom, trim the ends and press.

2 For the second border, join the 4½" I lengthwise strips in pairs with a diagonal seam. Use a short stitch (15 stitches per inch). Press seam open. Sew these borders to the sides. Trim the ends even with the quilt. Press the seams away from the quilt.

3 Sew the I borders to the top and bottom of the quilt. Cut the ends of the strips even with the edges of the quilt. Press the seams towards the border strips. See Figure 8 for the final layout of the crib quilt.

Lap Quilt

1 For the first splash fabric border, cut four of the 2" × 42" H strips in half. Sew a half strip to each of the remaining eight strips with a diagonal seam. Use a short stitch (15 stitches per inch). Press seams open. Sew borders to the sides of the quilt. Trim the ends even with the quilt. Press seams away from the quilt. Sew the H borders to the top and bottom, trim the ends, and press. The four remaining H borders are used later.

2 For the pieced border, sew together 2½" × 21" A, D and E strips in the order shown below to make a pieced band (Figure 9). Make three pieced bands. Press seam allowances in one direction. Re-cut the pieced bands into 2½" wide segments. You need a total of eighteen segments.

Figure 9

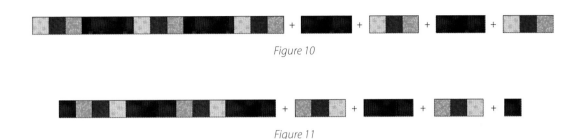

Figure 10

Figure 11

3 Following Figure 10, sew together five pieced rectangles and four fabric B rectangles to make a side border. Repeat. Sew to the sides of the quilt. Press seams away from the quilt. Trim ends even with the quilt if necessary.

4 Sew together four pieced rectangles and three B rectangles to make a border. Sew a 2½" B square at each end (Figure 11). Make two borders like this. Audition the border on the top of the quilt. If it is too long, take slightly larger seams between rectangles. If it's too short, re-stitch seams with narrower allowances. The H end squares should match the seams of the side borders exactly. Repeat for the bottom border. Press seams away from the quilt.

5 For the third splash fabric border, sew H borders leftover from step 1 to the sides. Trim ends even with the quilt, and press. Sew H borders to the top and bottom, trim, and press.

6 For the fourth splash fabric border, join the lengthwise strips in pairs with a diagonal seam. Use a short stitch. Press seam open. Sew the lengthwise strips to the sides of the quilt. Trim the ends even with the quilt. Press seams away from the quilt towards the border.

7 Join the I borders in pairs. Sew to the top and bottom of the quilt, trim and press.

QUILT AND BIND

NOTES FROM NANCY

If you need to keep your quilting projects portable, consider arranging the strips on a bath towel. If you don't get all the strips sewn together at one sewing session, roll up the towel. When it's time to sew again, unroll the towel—your strips will be in order!

quilts from leftovers

Well, here we are at the last chapter in the book and believe me, I have accumulated some leftover fabrics from these projects. You might ask, "So what's the difference between leftover fabrics and stash fabrics?" Stash fabrics haven't been cut or used. Leftover fabrics have already been used in other projects but still have enough left for future use.

I have a huge collection of bright fabrics that I use to make color wheels, and I wanted to create quilts that could use these leftovers. The quilt *Rings of Color* uses a combination of cool and warm fabrics set on a black background. The quilt gives the illusion of curves, but the pieces are really straight strips. I couldn't stop with only one quilt made with these bright colors, so I made *Crayon Box*—a very simple quilt but such fun to make.

Sometimes you just need a little of this or that to make a quilt like *Dancing Leaves*. Of all the quilts in the book, it is my favorite. It's hard to imagine that a block as humble as the Diamond in a Square can make such an impact on the overall design, but this block is actually what creates the large star. There are so many techniques in this quilt, and I truly hope you enjoy my flying geese border.

Another version of this quilt is *Garden Star*. The piecing is the same, but the splash fabric is what makes this quilt exceptional. There are always those certain fabrics that just seem to jump off the shelf and beg you to take them home. The splash fabric in *Garden Star* is one of those fabrics. The large floral fabric is cut out and fused down as the appliqué motifs in the Diamond in a Square blocks.

Simple piecing helps me to relax and relieve the stress of the day. I hope you find the same enjoyment making these quilts as I did.

Rings of Color

Pieced by: *Cindy Casciato*

Quilted by: *Cindy Casciato*

Quilt Sizes
Wall: 63" × 63" (shown)
Queen: 91" × 105"

Block Size: *7"*

I've been purchasing fabrics for color wheel patterns for years, so I have a lot of bright colors that I wanted to use for this quilt pattern. There are enough pattern pieces to use all twelve colors on the color wheel. You'll be surprised how easily this pattern comes together with simple strip piecing. Look through your stash for those blended prints that have a design on the surface but appear as one color for use in this quilt.

YARDAGE

FABRIC	WALL	FULL	FOR
Splash: Darkest print	2½ yds.	5¼ yds.	Background
Stash: 4 Warm prints (yellow-orange, orange, red-orange, red)	⅓ yd. each	½ yd. each	Ring Blocks
Stash: 4 Cool prints (yellow-green, blue, blue-green, blue-purple)	⅓ yd. each	½ yd. each	Ring Blocks
Stash: Warm print (yellow)	⅝ yd.	1¼ yds.	X Blocks
Stash: Cool print (green)	⅝ yd.	1¼ yds.	X Blocks
Stash: Transitional print (yellow-green)	½ yd.	1 yd.	X Blocks
Binding	⅝ yd.	1 yd.	
Backing	4 yds.	9½ yds.	

CUTS

FABRIC	WALL	FULL
Splash: Darkest print	Cut eleven strips 4" × 42"; re-cut into fifty-two rectangles 4" × 7 ½". Cut three strips 4¾" × 42"; re-cut into twenty 4¾" squares; re-cut twice on the diagonal for quarter-square triangles. Cut two strips 7½" × 42"; re-cut into nine 7½" squares.	Cut twenty-four strips 4" × 42"; re-cut into 119 rectangles 4" × 7 ½". Cut six strips 4¾" × 42"; re-cut into forty-six 4¾" squares ; re-cut twice on the diagonal for quarter-square triangles. Cut six strips 7½" × 42"; re-cut into thirty 7½" squares.
Stash: 4 Warm prints	Cut four strips 2¼" × 42" four each.	Cut seven strips 2¼" × 42" per fabric.
Stash: 4 Cool prints	Cut four strips 2¼" × 42" from each.	Cut seven strips 2¼" × 42" per fabric.
Stash: Warm print	Cut three strips 4½" × 42"; re-cut into forty rectangles 3" × 4½".	Cut seven strips 4½" × 42"; re-cut into ninety-two rectangles 3" × 4½".
Stash: Cool print	Cut three strips 4½" × 42"; re-cut into forty rectangles 3" × 4½".	Cut seven strips 4½" × 42" ; re-cut into ninety-two rectangles 3" × 4½".
Stash: Transitional print	Cut two strips 3" × 42"; re-cut into twenty 3" squares.	Cut four strips 3" × 42"; re-cut into forty-six 3" squares.

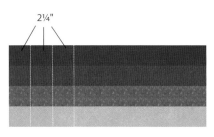

Figure 1

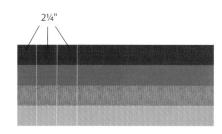

Figure 2

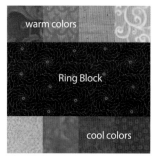

Figure 3

MAKE THE RING BLOCKS

1 Sew four warm color strips into a strip set from light to dark and four cool color strips into another set (Figures 1 and 2). Use a scant ¼" seam allowance. Make four sets of each color group for the wall quilt and seven sets for the queen quilt. Press the seams of the cool sets from dark to light. Press the seams of the warm sets from light to dark. The strip sets measure 7½" wide after piecing and pressing.

2 Cut across the strip sets every 2¼" (Figures 1 and 2). Each strip set yields seventeen sections. Make a total of fifty-two cool strip sections and fifty-two warm strip sections for the wall quilt. Make a total of 119 cool strip sections and 119 warm strip sections for the queen quilt.

3 Stack cool and warm sections into piles of ten each. Notice that the seam allowances are going in opposing directions. This will help to keep the final ring block squared up.

4 Sew a cool strip section to one long side of each 4" × 7½" background rectangle (Figure 3). Chain piece ten ring blocks at a time by feeding the sections under the needle end to end. Don't cut the threads in between the sections.

5 Turn the sections around and sew the warm strip section to the other side of each unit, turning sections so the dark and light fabrics are moving in the opposite direction to the cool colors (Figure 3).

6 Cut the threads when you complete ten ring blocks. Press the seam allowances away from the center section. Repeat the process until you have fifty-two ring blocks for the wall quilt and 119 for the queen quilt. Keep in mind that these units are used for the inside blocks and the pieced border.

MAKE THE X BLOCKS

1 Sew a transitional fabric (yellow-green) strip between two warm (yellow) strips (Figure 4). Make two strip sets for the wall quilt and four strip sets for the queen quilt. Press seams to the center strip.

2 Re-cut the strip set into 3" sections (Figure 4). Each strip set yields thirteen strip sections. Cut twenty sections for the wall quilt and forty-six sections for the queen quilt.

3 Make a stack of the 3" × 4½" cool (green) rectangles. Sew a dark quarter-square triangle to each long side of the cool rectangles, the right angles in the triangles matching the corner of the rectangle (Figure 5). Press the seams towards the triangles. Make forty triangle sections for the wall quilt and ninety-two triangle sections for the queen size quilt.

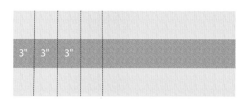

Figure 4

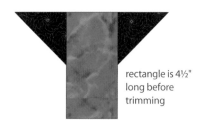

rectangle is 4½" long before trimming

Figure 5

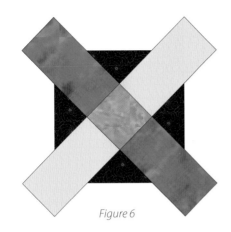

Figure 6

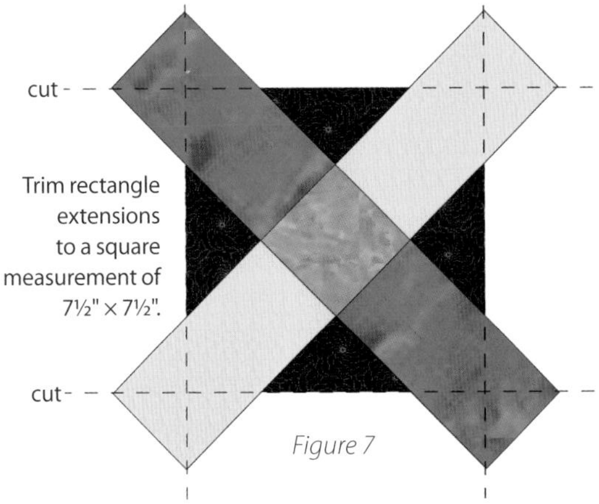

cut   cut

cut -

Trim rectangle
extensions
to a square
measurement of
7½" × 7½".

cut -

Figure 7

ASSEMBLE THE QUILT IN VERTICAL COLUMNS

Wall Quilt

1 The wall quilt has seven columns with seven blocks in each column. Next to your sewing machine, stack twenty-four ring blocks, sixteen X blocks, and nine dark 7½" squares

2 Make two columns that look like Figure 8, one column that looks like Figure 9, two columns that look like figure 10 and two columns that look like figure 11. Press all the seams toward the ring blocks.

Figure 8

Figure 9

Figure 10

Figure 11

4 Make a stack of ten of the transitional (yellow/yellow-green/yellow) strip sections. Sew a triangle section to each side of each transitional strip section. The seam allowances are already pressed in opposing directions to make joining this block simple. You can pin at the intersections if you like or try my method of using a stiletto or the pointed end of your trusty seam ripper (see page 15, step 3).

5 Chain-sew ten X blocks at a time by feeding the sections under the needle without breaking the threads in between the sections. Turn the sections around and feed the opposite side under the machine and add the other triangle section. Cut the threads when you complete ten X blocks. Repeat the process until you have twenty X blocks for the wall quilt and forty-six for the queen quilt (Figure 6).

6 Square up the X blocks to 7½" × 7½" (Figure 7).

Figure 12

Figure 13   *Figure 14*   *Figure 15*

3 Assemble the quilt top by joining the vertical columns using Figure 12 as a guide. The seam allowances are already pressed in opposing directions to make joining the rows simple. I recommend pinning at the intersections and using a stiletto or the point end of your seam ripper to hold the seams in place when you take out the pins to stitch.

Queen Quilt

1 The queen quilt has eleven columns with thirteen blocks in each column. Next to your sewing machine, stack seventy-one ring blocks, forty-two X blocks, and thirty dark 7½" squares.

2 Make five columns that look like Figure 13. You will flip two of the columns and start with the cool rings at the top of the quilt. Press all the seams toward the ring blocks.

3 Make three columns that look like Figure 14 and two columns that look like Figure 15. Press the seams toward the ring blocks.

4 Assemble the quilt top by joining the vertical columns using Figure 16 as a guide. I recommend pinning at the seam intersections and using a stiletto or the point end of your seam ripper to hold the seams in place when you take out the pins to stitch.

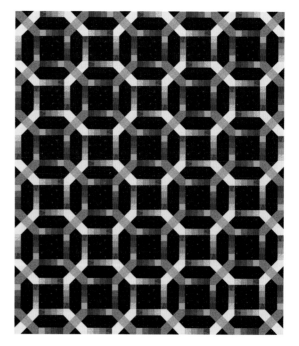

Figure 16

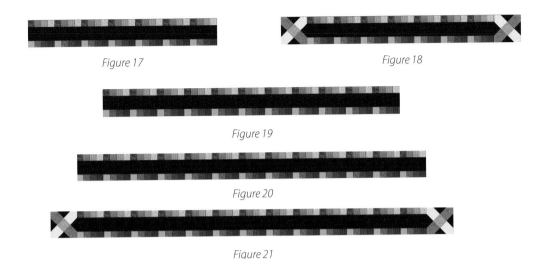

Figure 17

Figure 18

Figure 19

Figure 20

Figure 21

ASSEMBLE THE PIECED BORDER

Wall Quilt

1 Sew seven ring blocks to make a side border (Figure 17). Make two side borders. Sew on the two side borders.

2 Join seven ring blocks to make the top border. Sew an X block to each end (Figure 18). Look at the full size photo on page 100 to see the orientation of the X blocks. Make two borders like this.

3 Sew on the top and bottom borders. Match the corner intersections and then match the middle of the borders to the middle of the quilt. If you need to adjust the length of the border, do so by taking up or letting out extra seam allowance in the seams. See the project photo on page 100 for the final layout of the quilt.

Queen Quilt

1 Sew eleven ring blocks to make a top border (Figure 19). Make two borders like this. Sew on the top and bottom borders.

2 Join thirteen ring blocks to make a side border (Figure 20). Sew an X block to each end (Figure 21). Look at the full-size photo on page 100 to see the orientation of the X blocks. Make two borders like this.

3 Sew on the side borders. Match the corner intersections first, then find the middle of the quilt. If you need to adjust the length of the border, do so by taking up or letting out extra seam allowance in the seams. See Figure 22 for the final layout of the quilt.

QUILT AND BIND

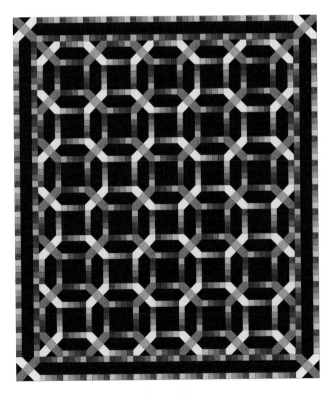

Figure 22

Garden Star

Quilt Size
Large Wall: 55" × 55"

Block Size: *12"*

This quilt is a smaller version of *Dancing Leaves*. You will utilize the motifs from a large floral print to create appliqués that compliment the overall quilt. I really enjoyed creating the floral designs by cutting out individual flowers within the floral print and rearranging them into groupings of appliqués. The simplicity of the blocks is deceiving and the end result of the finished quilt is quite a surprise. It's hard to find the individual blocks because the overall star design is what you see.

YARDAGE

FABRIC	WALL	FOR
Splash: Large floral print	2¼ yds.	Border and Appliqué Cutouts
Splash: Dark print (teal)	1¼ yds.	All Blocks, Flying Geese, Border Flap
Stash: Contrast print to complement flowers (gold)	5/8 yd.	Diamond in a Square Block Centers
Stash: Medium print (marble gold)	¼ yd.	Ohio Star Block
Stash: Lightest print (light gold)	¾ yd.	Diamond in a Square Blocks
Stash: Three red/orange prints	¼ yd. or a fat quarter for each	Flying Geese Border
Binding	½ yd.	
Backing	3½ yds.	
Steam-a-Seam 2 Lite Fusible Web	1 yd.	
Thin cotton batting (optional)	Nine 9" squares	3-D Appliqué

CUTS

FABRIC	WALL
Splash: Large floral print	Cut three strips 7" × 42" crosswise. Cut two strips 7" × remaining length of fabric. Set the rest of the fabric aside for the appliqué cut-outs.
Splash: Dark print (teal)	Cut five strips 1½ " × 42" for border flaps. Cut three strips 4" × 42"; re-cut into twenty-six 4" squares. Cut four 7" squares; recut into eight half-square triangles. Cut two 5½" squares. Cut four 4½" squares.
Stash: Contrast print (gold)	Cut two strips 9" × 42"; re-cut into eight 9" squares.
Stash : Medium print (marble gold)	Cut two 5½" squares. Cut one 4½" square.
Stash: Lightest print (light gold)	Cut three strips 7" × 42"; re-cut into twelve 7" squares; re-cut into twenty-four half-square triangles.
Stash: 3 Red/orange prints	Cut two 7½" squares from each. Cut two 4" squares from any fabric.
Binding	Cut seven strips 2¾" × 42".

MAKE THE OHIO STAR BLOCK

The Ohio Star block is a basic nine-patch grid, made with four background squares, one center square and four quarter-square triangle units.

1 Start the assembly process by making the quarter-square triangle units. Layer the 5½" dark squares right sides together with the 5½" accent squares. Follow the instructions in the Techniques section to make the four quarter-square units (pages 17-18). Press seams to the dark side. Ideally the quarter-square units should measure 4½".

2 Lay the completed quarter-square units and the 4½" square you cut out for the Ohio Star into a nine-patch grid (Figure1). Chain piece the units using the thread-pinning method. Stitch the squares together to form three horizontal rows.

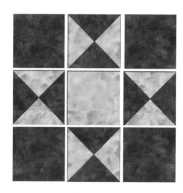

Figure 1

3 Sew the three rows together to make the block. The block should measure 12½" square. Don't worry if your block is smaller. The measurement for the Ohio Star block will determine the finished size to trim the Diamond in a Square blocks.

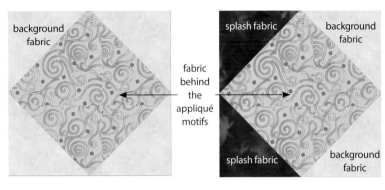

background fabric

splash fabric

background fabric

fabric behind the appliqué motifs

splash fabric

background fabric

Figure 2   *Figure 3*

MAKE THE DIAMOND IN A SQUARE BLOCKS

1 Refer to the instructions on aligning a diamond square (page 18). Fold the 9" center squares into quarters. Press the creases on the outside edges of the square.

2 Place the lightest half-square units right sides together with the squares. Align the points of the triangles with the crease lines in the squares.

3 Use the point of your seam ripper to hold down the triangle and keep the long edges together. Stitch a ¼" seam along the long edge.

4 Sew a light triangle to the opposite side of the square following the same method outlined above.

5 Place the pieced block with the triangle facing up on the ironing surface. Set the seam with the flat of the iron. Lift the triangles up and press away from the square.

6 Sew two more light triangles to the remaining sides of the square. Set seams and press triangles away from square (Figure 2). Make four A blocks like this.

7 Repeat these steps using two light triangles and two dark (teal) triangles for each block. Make four B blocks (Figure 3).

CREATE THE FLOWER APPLIQUÉS

1 Cut out individual floral motifs as you find them in your large scale floral. Try to find eight identical cut-outs of each of the appliqué motifs. You can choose one large motif or several smaller pieces to fit together. Keep the individual pieces in a separate stack. Continue cutting out the appliqués in a similar manner until you have enough to complete the eight blocks.

2 Cut a piece of Steam-a-Seam 2 Lite Fusible Web about 9" × 9". Remove one of the release papers from the fusible web to expose the tacky surface. Save this paper to use as a pressing sheet later.

3 Cut other pieces of fusible web about the size and shape of your rough-cut motifs. Remove one side of the release paper from the pieces of web. Smooth by hand the tacky surface of the fusible web to the back side of each motif. Do not remove the second release paper yet.

NOTES FROM **NANCY**

The Ohio Star pattern is very versatile! Switch colors for the center block for another option. Use the same color for the center as selected for the corner blocks. Or, choose a third fabric for the center block. Changing the fabric color is your prerogative!

4 Carefully cut out around the printed shapes. If you are cutting a complete large motif to use in each block, skip steps 5 and 6.

5 Remove the release paper from the back of the individual motifs. Place the cut-out motifs for one arrangement on the 9" square fusible web release paper. This magic paper acts just like an appliqué pressing sheet. Each appliqué piece will be tacky and you can stick it to the release paper. Arrange to your heart's content. Pretend you are creating a floral arrangement. Find a focus flower to begin. Add in some smaller flowers and leaves to support the main attraction. You decide how much is too much. Create the entire appliqué arrangement on the pressing sheet by slightly overlapping the individual pieces.

6 Once you are happy with the arrangement, steam press the individual motifs together. This will make the individual motifs into one whole appliqué piece. You can then remove the appliqué as a whole piece to transfer to your background block.

7 Repeat the steps above until you have an arrangement for each of the eight Diamond in a Square blocks and one for the quilt center.

STITCH THE APPLIQUÉ

1 Gently transfer the bouquets from the pressing sheet. Center the fusible appliqué flowers on the Diamond in a Square blocks and the center of the quilt. Fuse the flowers to the blocks (Figure 4).

Figure 4

Figure 5

2 Layer the appliqué block with a square of thin cotton batting. Pin baste with No. 2 safety pins.

3 Read 3-D Appliqué Method on pages 22-23. Select a decorative stitch on your machine such as a feather stitch or a zigzag stitch. Thread your machine with a 40/3 variegated thread that complements your motifs and stitch around them through the batting. Your bobbin thread can be any lightweight thread since it will not show on the quilt.

4 Turn the block over and trim the excess batting around the motif.

ASSEMBLE THE QUILT

1 Stitch the quilt together in horizontal rows, referring to Figure 5 for layout. Press seams open in each row. This will help you make the critical seam alignments necessary when each row is joined to make the quilt top.

2 Join the rows. Press the final seam allowances in one direction.

MAKE AND ADD THE FLYING GEESE BORDER

You need twenty-four flying geese units for the quilt border and four half-square units for the border corners.

1 Follow the instructions in the Techniques section for making flying geese (page 24). Use one 7½" square of geese (red/orange) fabric and four 4" teal squares to make four flying geese at a time. Make a total of twenty-four flying geese.

2 Join six flying geese units to make a pieced border, turning the red/orange triangles as shown in Figure 6 so the flying geese are all flying in the same direction. Make four borders like this.

Figure 6

Figure 7

3 Make four half-square units (see pages 16-17) with red/orange and teal 4" squares. Sew a half-square unit to opposing ends of two of these rows (Figure 7). Pay careful attention to the direction of the half-square units. Notice that the flying geese units are all pointing towards the center of the quilt. Keep in mind that the goose triangle is the bright colored triangle and the sky is the teal triangle on either side.

4 Sew the shorter side borders on first, making sure the geese are all pointing toward the center of the quilt. Press the seam allowance away from the center of the quilt toward the border.

5 Sew the top and bottom borders on next. Press seam allowances towards the flying geese border.

MAKE THE SECOND BORDER

This narrow flap border adds color between the flying geese border and the outer floral border. It is an inset like piping.

1 Cut one of the five teal 1½" × 42" strips in quarters. Stitch a quarter strip to one end of each of the four remaining strips. Join them with a diagonal seam and press the seam allowances open.

2 Press all four strips in half, wrong sides together. Set them aside to be added to the final border.

ADD THE SECOND AND THIRD BORDERS

1 It really helps to put the quilt top on a vertical flannel covered wall. Place the borders around the quilt and label them as top, bottom, right side and left side.

2 Cut one of the three crosswise floral border strips in half. Stitch half strips to one end of two crosswise borders. Matching centers, position a folded teal border on a long edge of each crosswise floral border, right sides together and raw edges even. Stitch the folded flaps to the floral borders using a narrow seam (Figure 8).

3 Position one of these borders right sides together along the side of the quilt. The flap is sandwiched in between. The raw edges of the border, the flap and the quilt should be even. Stitch the border/flap to the quilt. Be sure that the previous line of stitching from step 1 does not show on the front. Trim border/flap even with the sides of the quilt. Repeat for the bottom border.

4 Position and pin a folded flap to the side of the quilt, raw edges even, and with the unstitched flap extending about ½" past the top border flap. Fold back the end of the side flap even with the top border flap's folded edge and pin in place. Repeat this step on the other end of the flap.

5 Sew a lengthwise floral border to the side of the quilt, catching the flap in the seam. Press the side flap onto the floral border, pressing seam allowances toward the flying geese. Hand stitch the ends of the side border to hold in place. Trim the floral border even with the quilt. Repeat on the remaining side.

QUILT AND BIND

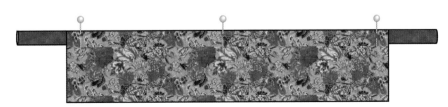

Figure 8

Dancing Leaves

Pieced by: *Cindy Casciato*

Quilted by: *Kay Wilson*

Quilt Sizes
Wall: 58" × 58"
Queen: 82" × 82" (shown)

Block Size: *12"*

Fall is in the air and dancing leaves are everywhere. Make a wall hanging or a queen size quilt and discover the secrets behind the seams. You will learn three of my techniques in this quilt: the 3-D Appliqué method, faster flying geese and the magic half-square tri-angle method. Once again, the simplicity of the blocks is deceiving—the end result is one large star with smaller stars within the overall design. This quilt goes together quickly and lends itself to many themes. Just picture the leaves as any theme that inspires you. Some of my students have cut out snowflakes and made a quilt all in blue and white. Others wanted to do summer theme. This quilt is limited only by your imagination.

YARDAGE

FABRIC	WALL	QUEEN	FOR
Splash: Leaf print	2 yds.	3¾ yds.	Borders, Setting Triangles and Diamond in a Square Blocks
Splash: Darkest print	2 yds.	3¼ yds.	Blocks, Flying Geese and Borders
Stash: Contrast print to complement leaves (tan)	¾ yd.	¾ yd.	Diamond in a Square Blocks
Stash: Lightest print (cream)	¾ yd.	¾ yd.	Diamond in a Square Blocks
Stash: Rust, red, orange, bronze or gold prints	¼ yd. or fat quarter for each of 6 prints	¼ yd. or fat quarter for each of 9 prints	Flying Geese, Ohio Star Blocks and Leaves
Binding	⅝ yd.	1 yd.	
Backing	3¾ yds.	7½ yds.	
Steam-a-Seam 2 Lite Fusible Web	1 yd.	1 yd.	
Thin cotton batting (optional)	Scraps	Scraps	

CUTS

FABRIC	WALL	QUEEN
Leaf print	Cut four strips 7" × length of fabric; cut one 7" square off the end of two of the border strips; re-cut squares into four half-square triangles.	Cut three strips 9½" × 42"; re-cut into eight setting triangles (see Techniques, page 12). Cut one strip 10½" × 42"; re-cut into two 10½"squares; re-cut into four half-square triangles; from remainder of strip cut two 7 "squares; re-cut each square into four half-square triangles. Cut four strips 10" × remaining length of fabric.
Darkest print	Cut six strips 2" × 42" (inner border). Cut one strip 5½" × 42 "; re-cut into two squares 5½"; re-cut remaining strip into four 4½" squares. Cut one strip 7" × 42"; re-cut into four squares 7"; re-cut into eight half-square triangles. Cut three strips 4" × 42"; re-cut into twenty-six 4" squares.	Cut fourteen strips 2" × 42". Cut three strips 4½" × 42"; re-cut into twenty 4½" squares. Cut two strips 5½" × 42"; re-cut into ten 5½" squares. Cut one strip 7" × 42"; re-cut into four squares 7"; re-cut into eight half-square triangles. Cut four strips 4" × 42"; re-cut into thirty-eight 4" squares.
Contrast print	Cut two strips 9" × 42"; re-cut into eight 9" squares.	Cut two strips 9" × 42"; re-cut into eight 9" squares.
Lightest print	Cut two strips 7" × 42"; re-cut into ten 7" squares; re-cut into twenty half-square triangles.	Cut two strips 7" × 42"; re-cut into ten 7" squares; re-cut into twenty half-square triangles.
Leaf prints	Cut one 7½" squares from each of six fabrics. Cut two 4" squares of one orange fabric. Cut two 5½" squares from one fabric. Cut one 4½" square from one fabric. Cut one rectangle 9" × 12" from each fabric (for appliqué leaves). Cut one 6" square from dark brown or wrong side of any leaf fabric.	Cut one 7½" square from each of nine fabrics. Cut two 4" squares of one orange fabric. Cut two 5½" squares from each of five fabrics. Cut one 4½" square from each of five fabrics. Cut one rectangles 9" × 12" from five fabrics (for appliqué leaves) Cut one 6" square from dark brown or wrong side of any leaf fabric (for stems).
Binding	Cut six strips 2¾" × 42".	Cut ten strips 2¾" × 42".

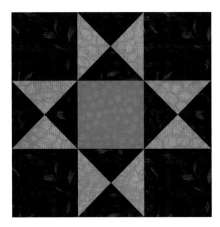

Figure 1

MAKE THE OHIO STAR BLOCKS

1 Follow instructions given on page 108 for *Garden Star*. Use 5½" dark squares and 5½" orange squares to make four units for the wall quilt and twenty quarter-square units for the queen quilt.

2 Refer to Figure 1 for the placement of units. Join the quarter-square units and 4½" squares to make five Ohio Star blocks for the queen quilt and one block for the wall quilt.

Figure 2

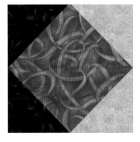

Figure 3

MAKE THE DIAMOND IN A SQUARE BLOCKS

Follow the instructions given on page 109 for Garden Star and the instructions in the Techniques section (page 18). Refer to Figures 2 and 3 for fabric placement. The center gold print is a 9" square. The corners are made with 7" half-square triangles. For either quilt, make four A blocks (Figure 2) and four B blocks (Figure 3).

CREATE THE LEAF APPLIQUÉS

There are five different leaf blocks that represent trees native to Ohio. Please feel free to put in leaves from trees in your state if you like.

Shagbark Hickory – Leaves are golden bronze

White Oak – Leaves are red

Buckeye Tree – Leaves are green

Silver Maple – Leaves are yellow and orange

Sweet Gum Tree – Leaves are gold

1 Follow the package directions and apply Steam-A-Seam 2 Lite fusible web to the back of each 9" × 12" red/brown/orange rectangle and to the back of the 6" squares (stems).

2 Trace the leaf templates that you would like to use on your quilt onto freezer paper. The templates are found on pages 118-119.

3 Remove one of the release papers from the fusible web to expose the tacky surface. Save this paper to use again later as a pressing sheet. Smooth by hand the tacky surface of the fusible web on to the wrong side of the fabric. Do not remove the second release paper from the backside just yet.

4 Cut out the freezer paper templates leaving each template with a margin of extra paper around the edges. Do not cut out the shape in detail just yet.

5 Press your freezer paper templates on the right side of the fabric sheets you have prepared with fusible web on the back.

6 Cut out a chunk of fabric around the freezer paper template from your fabric sheet. Do not cut out the detail shape just yet.

7 Do you need more than one of that particular leaf? You can cut two pieces at a time with accurate results. Just keep the pieces in a stack. Do not separate them.

8 Continue cutting out the rest of the leaf templates in a similar manner until you have all the leaves needed to complete the eight blocks.

9 Cut out stems directly from the fused fabric sheets. All the stems are around ¼" wide. Cut the stem strips across the diagonal direction of the fabric so they will have some flexibility.

STITCH THE APPLIQUÉ

1 See page 110 for tips on moving your motif. Arrange the leaves and stems on the center squares of the Diamond in a Square blocks. Fuse motifs in place.

2 Read 3-D Appliqué Method on pages 22-23. Layer the appliqué block with a square of cotton batting in a color such as warm and natural. Pin baste with No. 2 safety pins.

3 Select a decorative stitch on your machine such as a feather stitch or a zigzag stitch. Thread your machine with a 40/3 variegated thread that complements your leaves. Your bobbin thread can be any lightweight thread since it will not show on the quilt. Stitch around each motif through the batting.

4 Turn over the block and trim the excess batting around the leaves.

ASSEMBLE THE QUILT

1 Stitch the quilt together in three horizontal rows (Figure 4). Press seams open in each row. This will help you make the critical seam alignments necessary when joining rows.

2 Wall quilt: The next step is to make the flying geese units for the first border. Proceed to Making Flying Geese.

Queen quilt: The next step is to make the Ohio Star triangle corners.

MAKE OHIO STAR TRIANGLE CORNERS (QUEEN SIZE ONLY)

1 Re-cut each 7" × 42 " leaf print strip into three setting triangles with a 19" long side. Cut a total of eight triangles. See Cutting Out Setting Triangles on page 12 for details. The four large pieced corners are each made of an Ohio Star block surrounded by one smaller and two large setting triangles (Figure 5).

2 Match centers of the long edge of a 10½" leaf print half-square triangle with the top edge of the Ohio Star block. Sew the triangle to the block with a ¼" seam. Press the seam away from the block.

3 Add the two larger triangles to the two opposing sides of the block to create the large setting triangle. Press the seams away from the block (Figure 5).

4 Matching centers, sew a pieced corner to the top and bottom of the quilt. Trim the ends of the corner units even with the sides of the quilt.

5 Matching centers, sew a pieced corner to the two remaining sides. Trim the quilt so all sides are even using a large square acrylic ruler to ensure that the corners are square. See page 113 for a photograph of the finished queen quilt.

Figure 4

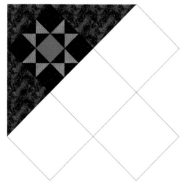

Figure 5

MAKE THE FLYING GEESE

Refer to page 24 for instructions on making the flying geese units for the quilts.

Wall quilt: Use twenty-four dark 4" squares and six medium 7½" squares to make twenty-four flying geese units. Use two dark 4" squares and two medium 4" squares to make four half-square triangle units for the corners of the flying geese border.

Queen quilt: Use thirty-six dark 4" squares and nine medium 7½" squares to make thirty-six flying geese units. Use two dark 4" squares and two medium 4" squares to make four half-square triangle units for the corners of the flying geese border.

ADD THE BORDERS

Wall Quilt

1 Join six flying geese units side by side to make a border. Make four borders like this.

2 Sew borders to the top and bottom of the quilt, adjusting fit if necessary by taking larger or smaller seam allowances between units. Press the seam allowances toward the quilt.

3 Sew a half-square unit to each end of the side borders. Sew to the quilt matching seams at the corners. Press the seam allowances toward the quilt.

4 Cut two dark 2" border strips in half. Sew a half-strip to the ends of each remaining strip. Sew a border to the top and bottom, trim ends even with the quilt and press borders away from the quilt. Sew borders to the sides, trim and press (Figure 6).

5 Stitch the outside leaf print borders to the quilt in the same order. See Figure 7 for an illustration of the complete wall quilt.

Queen Quilt

1 Cut two of the dark 2" border strips in half. Sew a half strip to an end of each of four full strips. Sew the borders onto the quilt following step 4 for the wall quilt.

2 Join nine flying geese units side by side to make a border. Make four borders like this.

3 Follow steps 2-3 for adding borders to the wall quilt. Sew flying geese borders to the queen quilt.

4 Join pairs of dark 2" border strips. Sew a border to the top and bottom, trim, and press away from the quilt. Sew borders to the sides, trim and press.

5 Add the 10" green leaf borders to the quilt in the same order, trimming after each addition. See the photo on page 113 for the complete queen quilt.

QUILT AND BIND

Figure 6

Figure 7

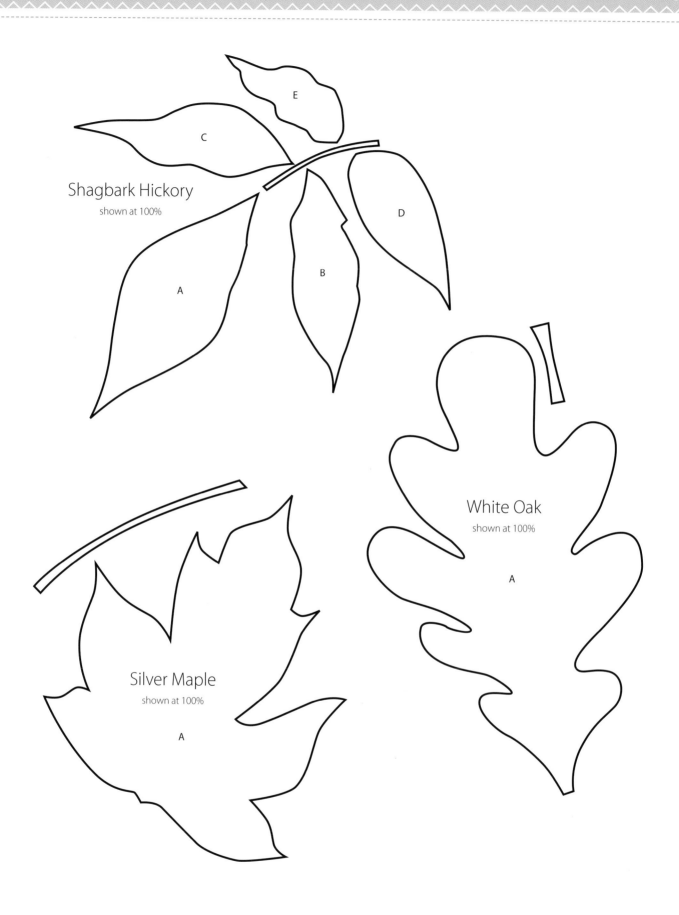

Shagbark Hickory
shown at 100%

White Oak
shown at 100%

Silver Maple
shown at 100%

Sweet Gum
shown at 100%

Buckeye Leaf
shown at 100%

Crayon Box

Pieced by: *Cindy Casciato*

Quilted by: *Janis Hittle*

Quilt Sizes
Queen: 88" × 109" (shown)
Lap: 60½" × 81¾"

Block Size: *15"*

The *Crayon Box* quilt is a quick strip project that utilizes a baker's dozen of your leftover stash fabrics. If you like to make quilts for charity or quilts that take you away from your daily stress, then this quilt is for you. This pattern allows you to put everything on remote control with easy assembly line piecing. You can make this quilt with any and every color in the rainbow or you can also choose a specific color palette and have just as much fun. The splash in this quilt is added with exciting background and border fabrics.

YARDAGE

FABRIC	LAP	QUEEN	FOR
Splash: Darkest print	1¾ yds.	2½ yds.	Setting Triangles
Splash	2½ yds.	3½ yds.	Outside Border
Stash: 13 contrasting fabrics in your choice of colors sorted into groups A–D (see Cuts Chart)	⅓ yd. each	⅝ yd. each	Color Blocks and Pieced Border
Stash	¾ yd.	1 yd.	Binding
Backing	5 yds.	10 yds.	

CUTS

FABRIC	LAP	QUEEN
Splash: Darkest print	Cut three strips 12" × 42". Cut two 12½" squares.	Cut five strips 12" × 42". Cut two 12½" squares.
Splash	Cut four strips 7" × length of fabric.	Cut four strips 10" × length of fabric.
Color Group A (4 fabrics)	* Cut two strips 3" × 42" from each; re-cut strips into 3" × 8" rectangles.	* Cut four strips 3" × 42" from each; re-cut strips into 3" × 8" rectangles.
Color Group B (6 fabrics)	* Cut two strips 3" × 42" from each; reserve two colors; re-cut four remaining color strips into 3" × 5½" rectangles.	* Cut three strips 3" × 42" from each; reserve two colors; re-cut four remaining color strips into 3" × 5½" rectangles.
Color Group C (2 fabrics)	* Cut three strips 3" × 42" from each; re-cut strips into 3" × 10½" rectangles.	* Cut six strips 3" × 42" from each; re-cut strips into 3" × 10½" rectangles.
Color Group D (1 fabric)	* Cut two strips 5½" × 42".	* Cut three strips 5½" × 42".
Stash	Cut eight strips 2¾" × 42".	Cut eleven strips 2¾" × 42".

* See Make the Pieced Stash Borders on pages 124-125 for more cutting information.

MAKE THE BLOCKS

Note: All seams are sewn with ¼" seam allowance.

1 Sew one 3" × 42" B strip to each of the long sides of the 5½" × 42" D strips. The strip panel should measure 10½" wide after sewing. Make three strip panels for the queen and two strip panels for the twin.

2 Re-cut the strip panels into 5½" wide segments. You will need a total of eighteen segments for the queen and eight segments for the twin. These are the center units for each block.

3 Stack the center units right side up beside your machine. Stack the 3" × 10½" C strips in two piles, one pile for each fabric. There should be eight strips in each pile for the twin quilt and eighteen strips in each pile for the queen quilt.

4 Place one center unit under your machine needle. Place a C strip right side down on top of the center unit, aligning the long sides from top to bottom. Stitch along the edge with a scant ¼" seam allowance.

5 Butt another center unit under the needle with a C strip aligned on top. Continue to guide the center units into the machine matching up with the C strips from one pile until all are sewn. Press the seams away from the center units.

6 Turn the units around and stitch the other C strip on the opposite side, creating a new square (Figure 1). Repeat on all units. The squares should measure 10½".

7 Make four stacks of B rectangles, each fabric in its own stack. The lap quilt will have eight strips in each stack. The queen quilt will have eighteen in each stack. Sew pairs of B rectangles together short end to short end from stacks 1 and 2. After pressing, the pieced strip should measure 10½" long. Sew pairs of B rectangles together from stacks 3 and 4. You should now have two piles of B pieced strip units, identical strips stacked together.

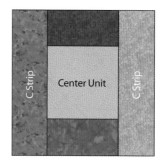

Figure 1

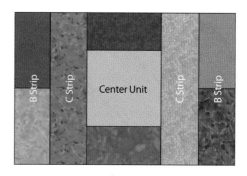

Figure 2

8 Stitch the B strip units on each side of the squares you completed in step 6. You should have eight new rectangle blocks (Figure 2).

9 Make four stacks of 3" × 8" fabric A strips, each stack with one fabric. There should be eight strips in each stack for the lap quilt and eighteen strips in each stack for the queen quilt.

10 Sew pairs of A strips together from stacks 1 and 2, and sew pairs together from stacks 3 and 4. Keep the two kinds of pieced strips in separate piles.

11 Stitch the A strip units to the top and bottom of the rectangles you completed in step 8 to form squares (Figure 3).

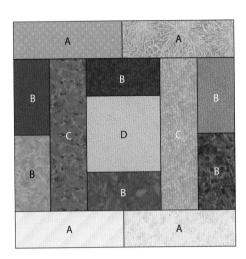

Figure 3

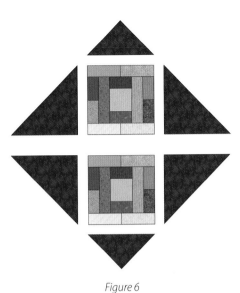

Figure 6

CUT OUT THE SETTING TRIANGLES

1 Refer to Cutting Out Setting Triangles (page 12). From each of the 12" × 42" dark strips, cut two triangles. Cut six triangles for the lap quilt and ten triangles for the queen quilt (Figure 4).

2 For either quilt, cut out two 12½" squares from the same dark print. Re-cut them in half on the diagonal (Figure 5). Mark the corners like the diagram in Figure 5. The triangles are sized to be generous. This allows for trimming and squaring the quilt once all rows are joined.

Figure 4

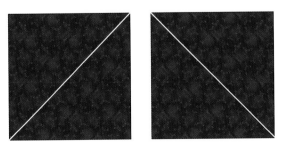

Figure 5

ASSEMBLE THE QUILT IN DIAGONAL ROWS

1 Arrange the blocks into diagonal rows. The lap quilt has four rows. The queen quilt has six rows.

2 Add a setting triangle to either side of the corner blocks to complete row 1 and row 4 for the lap quilt (Figure 6), or row 1 and row 6 for the queen quilt. Make each row the same. You will simply turn one around to create the opposite half of the quilt.

3 For the lap quilt, make two rows of three blocks side by side. Join the BB sides of the blocks. Add one setting triangle and one corner triangle to each end of the 3-block rows to complete rows 2 and 3. Make each row the same. You will simply turn them around to create the opposite half of the quilt. For the queen quilt, make two rows of three blocks side by side. Join the BB sides of the blocks. Add two setting triangles to the ends of the 3-block rows to complete rows 2 and 5. Make each row the same. You will simply turn one around to create the opposite half of the quilt.

4 For the queen quilt only: Make two rows of five blocks side by side. Join the BB sides of the blocks. Add one setting triangle and one corner triangle to the ends of the 5-block rows to complete rows 3 and 4. Make each row the same. You will simply turn one around to create the opposite half of the quilt.

Instead of setting the Crayon Blocks on point, another option is to create rows and columns.

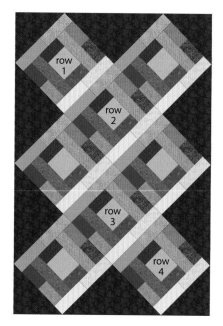

Figure 7

5 Join the diagonal rows to make two identical halves of the quilt. The lap quilt will have two rows per half and the queen will have three rows per half. Join the halves to complete the top (Figures 7 and 8).

6 Press the quilt from the back and from the front. Trim the edges of the quilt evenly, being sure to leave a generous ¼" seam allowance beyond the points of the blocks. Square up the corners.

MAKE THE PIECED STASH BORDERS

Lap Quilt

1 Cut twenty-six 3" × 5½" rectangles from seven different stash fabrics.

2 Sew thirteen rectangles together, short end to short end to make a side border. Press seam allowances in one direction. If it is too long, take slightly larger seam allowances between fabrics as needed. Sew to the side of the quilt. Repeat for the other side, changing the order of the fabrics.

3 Cut eighteen 3" × 5½" rectangles from five different stash fabrics.

4 Cut four corner squares 3" × 3" from a different fabric.

5 Sew nine rectangles together, short end to short end to create the top border. Repeat for the bottom border, changing the order of the fabrics. Sew a corner square to each end of the top and bottom borders.

Figure 8

6 Sew the four corner squares to each end of the top and bottom borders.

7 Fit the top and bottom borders to the quilt by pinning in place. If you need to adjust the length of the border, take in or let out the seam allowances. Sew borders to the top and bottom of the quilt.

Queen Quilt

1 Cut ten 3" × 17½" rectangles from five different stash fabrics.

2 Sew five rectangles together, short end to short end to create one side border. Sew to the side of the quilt. Trim ends even with the edges of the quilt. Repeat for the other side border, changing the order of the fabrics.

3 Cut ten 3" × 13½" rectangles from five different stash fabrics.

4 Sew five rectangles together, short end to short end to create the top border. Repeat for the bottom border, changing the order of the fabrics.

5 Cut four corner squares 3" × 3" from a different fabric. Sew a corner square to each end of the top and bottom borders.

6 Fit the top and bottom borders to the quilt by pinning in place. If you need to adjust the length of the border, take in or let out the seam allowances. Sew borders to the top and bottom of the quilt (Figure 9).

ADD THE FINAL SPLASH BORDER

1 Starting with the long sides, pin border strips to the quilt. Sew border strips to the quilt. Trim the strip border even with the edge of the quilt.

2 Pin the top and bottom borders in place and then sew the borders to the quilt. Press seam allowances towards the borders. See Figure 10 for the final layout of the lap quilt. See the project photo on page 121 for the final layout of the queen quilt.

QUILT AND BIND

Figure 9

Figure 10

Resources

These are some of my favorite tools that I use constantly in my studio and whenever I'm out teaching.

June Tailor's Get Squared Ruler

Wright's EZ Flip n' Set Ruler

Creative Grid's Setting Triangle Ruler

Warm Company's Warm and Natural Batting

Warm Company's Steam-a-Seam 2 Light Fusible Web

Magic Triangle ⅜" Marking Tool from Cindy Casciato

Little Foot's ¼" and ⅜" Presser Foot

Jenkins' Necktie Company Printable Freezer Paper

Olfa's 60mm Rotary Cutter

Rowenta Irons

Kay Wilson (Kay's Frugal Fabrics)
549 Campbell Rd.
Ghent, KY 41045
wilsondkjb@aol.com

Quilting by Nancy Gano
3936 Alliance Rd.
Rootstown, OH 44272
330-654-0834
ncygano@yahoo.com

Quilting by JoAnne West (JoAnne's Custom Quilts)
5079 St. Rt. 14
Ravenna, OH 44266
330-285-2836

Quilting by Eva Birch (Stitch by Stitch Creations)
4893 Lake Rockwell Rd.
Ravenna, OH 44266
330-297-9968
Evaexcel13@yahoo.com

Quilting by Janis Hittle
7881 St. Rt. 88
Ravenna, OH 44266
330-297-9286
janhittle@aol.com

Index

Keep creating with Nancy!

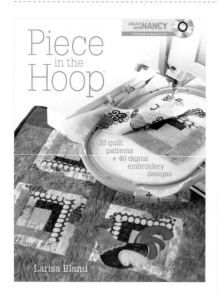

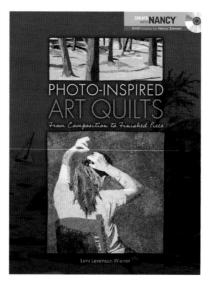

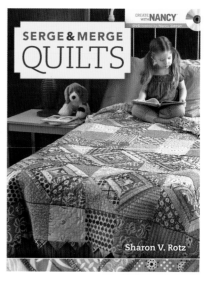

Piece in the Hoop™

20 quilt projects + 40 machine embroidery designs

Larisa Bland and Nancy Zieman

Turn your embroidery machine into a block-piecing machine! With Larisa's designs, you can piece in the hoop™! All you have to do is add fabric and flip—the embroidery machine does all the sewing for you. This method results in fast, precise blocks every time!

paperback; 8.25" × 10.875"; 128 pages

ISBN-10: 1-4402-0356-3

ISBN-13: 978-1-4402-0356-5

SRN: Z4957

Photo-Inspired Art Quilts

From Composition to Finished Piece

Leni Levenson Wiener and Nancy Zieman

Starting with nothing but fabric and a favorite photo, learn to create beautiful art quilts. Author and art quilter Leni Levenson Wiener gives you the tools you need for the entire process—from composition to bound and finished piece—to help you develop your own artistic voice.

paperback; 8.25" × 10.875"; 128 pages

ISBN-10: 0-89689-804-0

ISBN-13: 978-0-89689-804-2

SRN: Z2873

Serge and Merge Quilts

Sharon V. Rotz and Nancy Zieman

Learn how to use standard serging stitches to neatly construct and creatively embellish quilts—from old-fashioned scrap quilts to sophisticated wall-hangings. You don't have to be an expert at serging (or quiltmaking!) to get great results.

paperback; 8.25" × 10.875"; 128 pages

ISBN-10: 0-89689-810-5

ISBN-13: 978-0-89689-810-3

SRN: Z2917

These and other fine Krause Publications titles are available at your local craft retailer, bookstore or online supplier, or visit our website at www.mycraftivitystore.com.